Best of Scandinavian Cooking

Best of Scandinavian Cooking

Danish, Norwegian and Swedish

**SHIRLEY SARVIS &
BARBARA SCOTT O'NEIL**

*Illustrated by
Barbara Scott O'Neil*

HIPPOCRENE BOOKS
New York

Originally published 1963 by Doubleday & Company, Inc.

Hippocrene paperback edition, 1997.
Second paperback printing, 2000.

For information, address:
HIPPOCRENE BOOKS, INC.
171 Madison Avenue
New York, NY 10016

Library of Congress Cataloging-in-Publication Data
Sarvis, Shirley.
      Best of Scandinavian cooking / Shirley Sarvis & Barbara Scott
O'Neil; illustrated by Barbara Scott O'Neil.
         p. cm.
      Includes index.
      ISBN 0-7818-0547-3
        1. Cookery, Scandinavian. I. O'Neil, Barbara Scott. II. Title.
TX722.A1S24   1997
641.5948--dc21   96-53545
                                    CIP

Printed in the United States of America.

*Dedicated to the generous Scandinavians
who shared their secrets of home cooking.*

TABLE OF CONTENTS

INTRODUCTION

Once, when it was summer, two young ladies of San Francisco (one a food editor, one a teacher) took their healthy, discriminating appetites and set out for Scandinavia. There they hoped to eat wonderful foods, meet the smiling Nordic people, and explore the countryside—then capture it all in a travel cookbook. Scandinavia, in their minds, was a fascinating blend of smooth-skinned blonds and copper spires, winter sports and Grieg, cheeses and Ingmar Bergman, bicycles, blue pottery, and pastries.

We are those young ladies. With great excitement and optimism, we clambered aboard a plane for Copenhagen.

Once there, we planned to toss our belongings into the car awaiting us and start immediately on a tour of Denmark. We perused our travel books and maps, circled towns that sounded enticing, then sketched a vague route through them—a carefree wiggly path that began in Denmark, went up through Sweden, across to Norway, and back to Stockholm again.

Among our assorted baggage were art pads, typewriter, and two billowy green sleeping bags. We hoped the Scandinavians would not be too alarmed by the sight of two young wanderers camping in their fields. We wanted ours to be a relaxed and unhurried trip, with time between eating and recipe interviews for picnics and berrypicking, art museums and concerts.

We wondered how it would all transpire. During the restless hours of our economy flight, we confessed shared misgivings that we might return plumper and wiser, but sadly lacking in material to present to the formidable New York publishers.

As soon as we landed, we plunged into the tasting part of our venture. We raced to a Copenhagen pastry shop to sample real Danish pastry. . . . And what glorious morsels we savored! There followed a primary tasting of an ingenious *smørrebrød;* soon after—a delicate omelet.

With any fears of a shortage of good food thus allayed, we set out in a search for the best to be had in fine home cooking. Our plan was to ask for favorite recipes from the ladies known to be the grandest cooks wherever we went.

That we did. All summer long, we sampled our way through the kitchens of the best home cooks in Scandinavia. And all summer long, we existed in that state of rapture that comes from blissful eating.

Guided sometimes by the tourist-agency officer, sometimes by a policeman, perhaps by the mayor, a food vendor, a newspaper editor, a shopkeeper, we tracked down the prize cooks. They turned out to be farmers' wives, society hostesses, grandmothers, young brides, even a gourmet bachelor.

Sometimes we discovered culinary wizards on our own— by trailing a lady shopper in a bustling open-air market as she fastidiously picked out food for her family's table; by seeking out the wife of a well-fed-looking husband; by hopefully querying a ferryboat companion just because she *looked* like a good cook.

We talked to cooks over coffee. We chatted with them in their kitchens. We watched them cook, letting demonstrations explain what dissimilar languages couldn't. We sat by the hour, spellbound, as a grandmother told how to cook the dishes her children liked most. We took notes in feverish excitement as a well-to-do Stockholm widow described her most exquisite party fare.

We found ourselves munching irresistible things to eat as proud homemakers thrust upon us samples of their skills. Before only dreams, such glories as Norwegian Blueberry Omelet, Danish Butter Cake, Nut-stuffed Burgundy Ham Rolls now became recipe realities.

Perpetually surrounded by tastes and tales of good food, our only despair was the constant fear of added poundage. But we soon eradicated even that, reassured by a buoyant Dane—"You'll have something to show for your trip."

We luxuriated in the warmth of the Scandinavians' welcome. A drenching of hospitality they poured upon us. Once we described our cookbook project to a young salesgirl in a Norwegian department store; she invited us to her family's home for dinner the next night. We registered discreet interest in the menu for a Danish Sunday dinner, and moments later sat in a sunny farm kitchen, watched dinner preparations, and shared in the tasting of it.

The more we got acquainted with Scandinavian cuisine, the more we postulated theories about what makes it so good:

Scandinavians like to eat—and eat well. The pursuit of good food absorbs a lot of their attention and energy—which they happily give. There is no conversational topic they approach with more devotion, no leisure activity more time-consuming.

Home cooking in Scandinavia is a family scheme. A good recipe lasts through many generations. Just as mothers skillfully interlocked simple flavors to make something remarkable to eat, so do their daughters. Scandinavians know they like the good food they've always enjoyed. Innovations are secondary.

Scandinavian housewives shop *daily* (but at least as much for the sociability as to get the freshest groceries).

It is no mistaken image that cream and eggs and butter and sugar characterize the richness and wholesomeness of Scandinavian repasts. And add to that their abundant fresh fruits and vegetables, rich grains and cereals, excellent seafood, and choice meats.

At the end of our adventures, we were convinced of an undeniable correlation between the Scandinavians' collective good spirits and their magnificent food.

But an unsolved quandary we yet ponder: Which came first—the jovial cooks who made the food so good it made the people happy? Or the good food that made the cooks so happy they made the food good?

Later, back in San Francisco, we carefully cooked and tested and retested every dish. We simplified preparations and adjusted ingredients, measurements, and utensils to suit American standards. We chose the finest recipes to share with you.

DANISH DIVERTISSEMENTS

Snugly packed into our small pistachio-green car, we headed for the Danish farmlands to the south of Copenhagen. We stopped for dinner at a tiny roadside inn. No one spoke English. Barbara drew a  , the innkeeper smiled knowingly, and within minutes returned with a tasty platterful of fish.

At dusk, we started off again. A short drive along a tree-fringed road brought us to the tidy farm village of Store Heddinge. Just as we were wondering how to get permission to sleep in the lush, green fields, we came across a wholesome-looking couple out for an evening stroll. Mr. Olsen, an endearing soul with wispy hair and sturdy high-heeled clogs, said "of course" we could roll out our sleeping bags and spend the night in the nearby clover patch.

Next morning, Mrs. Olsen hailed us, invited us for "coffee," and soon we were munching a bountiful breakfast at a corner table in the garden! As conversation turned to food, Mrs. Olsen blossomed. We had found a noteworthy cook with whom to begin our recipe search.

When she's cooking especially to please her nineteen-year-old son, Mrs. Olsen puts a young beef tongue on to simmer, and later serves it sliced and steaming under a mushroom-sherry sauce. Sometimes she adds a melted herb-butter sauce.

SLICED TONGUE WITH MUSHROOM-SHERRY SAUCE

1 *small beef tongue (about*	*Boiled whole carrots, peas,*
2½ pounds)	*cauliflower, and small po-*
Water	*tatoes*
1½ *teaspoons salt*	½ *pound fresh mushrooms,*
2 *bay leaves*	*sliced*
3 *peppercorns*	¼ *cup (½ stick) butter*
1 *small onion, sliced*	2 *tablespoons dry sherry*

Place washed tongue in kettle; cover with water. Add salt, bay leaves, peppercorns, and onion. Cover kettle and simmer tongue 2½ hours or until very tender when pierced with a fork. Trim excess tissue from root end and remove skin. Slice tongue and arrange on a heated platter, surrounded by cooked carrots, peas, cauliflower, and potatoes; keep warm. Sauté mushrooms in butter just until tender. Add sherry and heat through. Pour sauce over tongue slices. *Makes 6 servings.*

Variation: Follow directions above, but do not make mushroom sauce. Instead, serve tongue with sauce of ½ cup (1 stick) butter and ⅛ teaspoon crumbled dried marjoram heated together just until butter is bubbling and slightly browned.

It's a good cook's privilege to make her own improvements on any classic recipe. Mrs. Olsen takes liberties with famed Danish *Bøf* (fried steak with onions), and makes an admirable new dish of pork. An extended embellishment—a cool, fresh rhubarb-and-red-raspberry relish.

BUTTER-BROWNED PORK TENDERLOIN AND ONIONS

2 large onions, thinly sliced	*tenderloin, pounded into*
¼ cup butter	*steaks less than ½-inch*
Salt	*thick*
Pepper	*Flour*
Dried marjoram	*Butter (if necessary)*
1½ pounds boneless pork	

In a large frying pan, slowly sauté onions in butter, stirring, for 30 minutes or until golden brown and slightly crisp; season onions with a little salt and pepper and a pinch of crumbled dried marjoram. Remove from frying pan; keep warm. Season both sides of tenderloin steaks with salt and pepper and a very small amount of crumbled dried marjoram. Coat with flour. Add a small amount of butter to frying pan if necessary. Over medium heat, brown meat, cooking about 4 minutes on each side. Arrange steaks on heated serving platter; top with browned onions. Serve with Red Raspberry-Rhubarb Relish (following). *Makes 4 servings.*

Note: When you purchase meat for this recipe, ask your meat man to cut boneless pork tenderloin into butterfly steaks, then pound them very thin.

Though especially designed to go with pork, this relish is impartial enough to complement chicken, too.

RED RASPBERRY-RHUBARB RELISH

1 *pound fresh rhubarb, cut into ½-inch pieces*	1½ *cups fresh red raspberries (or 1 package, about 10-*
1 *cup sugar*	*ounce size, frozen rasp-*
1 *tablespoon water*	*berries in heavy syrup)*
2 *teaspoons lemon juice*	1 *to 2 teaspoons vinegar*
Few grains of salt	

Combine in a saucepan rhubarb, sugar, water, lemon juice, and salt. Cook over low heat, stirring occasionally, until rhubarb is barely tender. Drain rhubarb; save syrup. Measure ¼ cup of the syrup and return to saucepan. (Store remaining syrup for another use.) Add raspberries and cook just until tender (or thawed). Drain raspberries. Gently combine raspberries with drained rhubarb. Add vinegar. Chill thoroughly. *Makes about 1½ cups relish.*

As we were finishing breakfast in the Olsen's yard, Farmer Nielsen's chubby daughter bicycled by. She said we could all watch her mother (the best cook in the countryside, according to Mrs. Olsen) make Sunday chicken dinner. We hurried off to follow her.

As we entered the kitchen, we sniffed sweet strawberries plumping in sugar syrup for jam-making the next day. But on the shining wooden counter lay promise of good food to come that day—a plucked and cleaned roasting chicken. We were enchanted by the happy atmosphere—Mrs. Nielsen bustling around, the daughter puffing in a trail behind her.

But before dinner came morning coffee, cakes, and cookies on the lawn. And Mrs. Nielsen rushed out with her specialty, Wales Bread, whipped up on the spot.

No less than twenty full minutes were carefully counted, open kitchen windows were whirled shut, and the outside door closed tightly before we dared peek at the baking Wales Bread. Without these precautions, the light and puffy pastry layers would "fall together," explained Mrs. Nielsen.

Mrs. Nielsen's Wales Bread is essentially cream puff paste —*pâté à chou*. Her use of it makes the difference: She smooths it into a wide strip to border an oblong pan for baking. Afterward she decorates with drizzles of powdered-sugar icing and swirls of homemade red currant jelly.

MRS. NIELSEN'S WALES BREAD
(*Cream Puff Coffee Bread*)

1 cup water	1 teaspoon vanilla
½ cup (1 stick) butter	About 1 tablespoon cream or
⅛ teaspoon salt	milk
1 cup flour	About ¾ cup red currant
4 eggs	jelly
1 cup sifted powdered sugar	

In a saucepan, heat water, butter, and salt until butter melts and mixture boils. Sift flour, measure, and add all at once to boiling liquid. Stir briskly over low heat until dough leaves sides of pans and forms a mixture that does not separate, about 1 minute. Allow mixture to cool a few minutes. Add eggs, one at a time, beating thoroughly after each addition until mixture is smooth and satiny. Spread dough around outside edge of a well-greased oblong baking pan (about 11 by 15 inches), making a strip about 3 inches wide and ½-inch thick. Bake in a moderately hot oven (375°) for 40 minutes or until crisp and golden brown. Allow to cool on a wire rack away from draft. Stir together powdered sugar, vanilla, and enough cream to make a thin icing. When bread is cool, drizzle icing in a pattern down center of the bread ring. Top with a pattern of red currant jelly piped through a plain-tipped cloth force bag (or make one yourself, forming a cone of waxed paper or parchment). Slice bread into wide strips to serve with coffee. *Makes 12 generous servings.*

For morning coffee, there also came forth a light yellow cake with a candy-like penuche topping that crinkled between the whole almonds each time one of us sliced a portion.

ALMOND CANDY-TOPPED COFFEE CAKE

1½ cups all-purpose flour	1 cup heavy cream
1 cup sugar	2 eggs
2 teaspoons baking powder	1 teaspoon vanilla
½ teaspoon salt	

Almond candy frosting:

⅓ cup butter	½ cup whole unblanched
⅔ cup brown sugar, firmly	almonds
packed	3 tablespoons milk
	1½ cups sifted powdered
	sugar

Sift flour, measure, and sift again with sugar, baking powder, and salt. In a mixing bowl, whip cream until stiff; beat in eggs and vanilla. Add sifted dry ingredients to cream mixture and beat until thoroughly blended. Pour batter into a greased 9-inch round cake pan. Bake in a moderate oven (350°) for 45 minutes or until cake begins to pull away from edge of pan and toothpick inserted in center comes out clean. Let cake stand 10 minutes, turn out on wire rack, allow to cool. To make frosting, melt butter in saucepan and stir in brown sugar and almonds. Slowly bring mixture to a boil and cook over low heat, stirring constantly, for 2 minutes. Add milk and continue to cook, stirring constantly, until mixture comes to a boil. Remove from heat; cool to lukewarm. Gradually add powdered sugar, and beat until frosting is of a good spreading consistency. Spread over top of cooled cake; allow to drizzle down sides. *Makes 10 servings.*

But at the Nielsens', just cake and Wales Bread would never do for "something to go with coffee." Heaped before us were rounds of white bread thickly spread with butter,* sweet currant-studded wafers, and crisp Danish lace cookies.

* "Tooth butter," the Danes call it. (Butter is applied so thickly, you can see your tooth marks when you bite into it.)

These cookies are butterscotch-flavored—with a hint of orange.

ORANGE LACE COOKIES

½ cup flour
½ cup sugar
¼ teaspoon baking powder
½ cup quick-cooking oatmeal
⅓ cup melted butter
2 tablespoons heavy cream

2 tablespoons light corn syrup
2 teaspoons vanilla
1 teaspoon almond extract
1 teaspoon finely grated orange peel

Sift flour, measure, and sift again into mixing bowl with the sugar and baking powder. Add oatmeal, butter, cream, syrup, vanilla, almond extract, and orange peel. Stir to blend thoroughly. Using a ¼-teaspoon measuring spoon for size, drop dough onto ungreased baking sheet, spacing cookies 4 inches apart. Bake in a moderately hot oven (375°) for 6 to 8 minutes. Let cookies cool a few seconds. As soon as they become slightly firm, loosen and lift them to a wire rack to cool, using a flexible spatula. *Makes about 6 dozen cookies.*

The time had come for Sunday dinner. We sat in the kitchen and ate a hearty meal, trying to express our appreciation in Danish by gesture and grateful sighs. What thoughtful people! What good food—and so early in our travels. (We couldn't wait to tell those skeptics at home.)

Mrs. Nielsen had stuffed the chicken full of fresh parsley sprigs, and browned and stewed it in butter. But the taste results defied such ease of preparation.

PARSLEY CHICKEN STEWED IN BUTTER

1 whole chicken (3 to 4 pounds)	2 tablespoons flour
Salt	About 1½ cups water
1 bunch fresh parsley	1½ teaspoons sugar
½ cup (1 stick) butter	Salt
	Pepper

Rinse chicken; pat dry; rub cavity lightly with salt. Stuff cavity full of parsley sprigs. Tie shut. Melt butter in a heavy kettle or large saucepan with tight-fitting cover. Add whole trussed chicken. Over medium heat, brown chicken thoroughly on all sides. When chicken is brown, cover kettle. Reduce heat, and simmer chicken 50 minutes or until very tender. Remove chicken from kettle. With poultry shears, cut it into serving pieces. Arrange pieces on heated serving platter, with parsley piled together at one end of platter; keep warm. Make sauce: Loosen drippings remaining in bottom of pan; heat to bubbling. Gradually stir in flour to make a smooth paste. Gradually add water, cooking and stirring sauce until smooth. Stir in sugar. Taste; add salt and pepper to correct seasoning. Serve sauce with chicken (and perhaps boiled new potatoes). *Makes 6 servings.*

We discovered the ecstasy of eating fresh lettuce plucked from the garden—tossed with a sweet whipped-egg dressing.

LETTUCE SALAD WITH WHIPPED EGG DRESSING

2 *eggs, separated*	1 *head butter lettuce, washed*
¼ *cup sugar*	*and thoroughly drained*
2 *tablespoons vinegar*	*and dried*
1 *tablespoon heavy cream*	1 *tomato, thinly sliced*

Beat egg whites until stiff but not dry; set aside. Beat egg yolks with sugar until thick and light-colored. Beat in vinegar and cream. Tear lettuce leaves into chilled salad bowl. Just before serving, fold egg whites into yolk mixture and pour the dressing over lettuce; toss gently. Cut each tomato slice in half and arrange over top of salad. *Makes 4 servings.*

June is the season for strawberries in Denmark. The Danes probably like them best unadulterated—except for cream and a swishy sounding sprinkling of coarse granulated sugar. But June strawberries also make the best *Rødgrød* (red-berry pudding). Mrs. Nielsen's is exceptional; its added enhancement is the fruit syrup from garden rhubarb, sugared and cooked. She calls it "Strawberry Porridge." We tasted it dipped from a huge glass bowl into wide soup bowls, and swimming in the morning's fresh milk, streaked with cream.

STRAWBERRY PORRIDGE
(Rødgrød)

1 *quart strawberries, washed*	¾ *cup sugar*
and stemmed	2 *tablespoons water*
¾ *cup sugar*	2½ *tablespoons cornstarch*
½ *cup water*	4 *tablespoons water*
Few grains of salt	2 *teaspoons lemon juice*
1 *pound rhubarb, cut into*	*Cold cream or milk*
1-inch pieces	

Combine in a saucepan the strawberries, sugar, ½ cup water, and salt. Heat, stirring occasionally, just until mixture boils. Remove from heat; set aside for about 30 minutes. Meantime combine rhubarb, sugar, and 2 tablespoons water in a saucepan. Cook over medium heat, stirring occasionally, until rhubarb is tender, about 20 minutes. Drain 1 cup syrup from rhubarb; reserve. Store remaining rhubarb and syrup for another use. Combine the 1 cup rhubarb syrup with strawberries. Heat to boiling. Stir together cornstarch and the 4 tablespoons water. Stir into fruit. Cook and stir a few minutes until fruit sauce thickens and becomes clear. Remove from heat; stir in lemon juice. Allow sauce to cool; chill. Serve with cream or milk. *Makes 6 servings.*

Replete, we went back to the Olsens' to collect our luggage and be on our way. Mr. Olsen printed a large sign (in Danish) for our future use: "MAY WE SLEEP IN YOUR FIELD THIS NIGHT?" As we drove off, he said we were always welcome, that we had "amused" them . . . they hoped someday to see a copy of our "bestseller" . . . did we have enough petrol? . . . did we leave any belongings behind in our "bedroom"?

A photograph of dazzling white chalk cliffs lured us to the Isle of Møn, a small island off the southern coast of Zealand.

Lashed by blusterous winds, we stumbled from our hotel down a steep descent to the water, determined to have a picnic. Half-encased in sleeping bags, we struggled with excess goodies gathered up at the close of the usual extensive Coffee "Complet"—sandy bits of cheese and bread and butter (smuggled out of the dining room via an eggshell). Soon the wind turned to rain, and we were huffing our way up 400 feet worth of chalk cliff to return to a contrasting delight—the shelter of our hotel and a description of an exquisite cake.

The lemony butter cake pushes its way upward to settle between the apple slices as the cake bakes.

APPLE CAKE
FROM THE ISLE OF MØN

½ cup (1 stick) butter
½ cup sugar
2 eggs
1 teaspoon grated lemon peel
1 teaspoon lemon juice
1 cup all-purpose flour

5 medium-sized cooking apples, peeled and thinly sliced
About 2 tablespoons melted butter
About 2 tablespoons sugar

Topping:
1 cup heavy cream
3 tablespoons sugar
½ teaspoon vanilla

In a mixing bowl, cream together butter and sugar until light and fluffy. Beat in eggs, one at a time. Add lemon peel and juice. Sift flour, measure, and gradually add to butter mixture; beat until smooth. Turn cake batter into bottom of a greased 9- or 10-inch springform pan. Arrange apple slices evenly over batter. Lightly brush top apple slices with melted butter; sprinkle with sugar. Bake in a moderate oven (350°) 1 hour. Allow cake to cool a few minutes. Meanwhile whip cream with sugar and vanilla. Remove cake-pan sides. Cut cake in wedges and serve warm. Top each serving with a generous spoonful of the whipped cream. *Makes 8 servings.*

A bobbing ferryboat carried us from Zealand to Funen. There, in the seaside town of Nyborg, we took time out from pastryshop snooping to bicycle to the historic Nyborg Castle, a real fairy-tale vision, complete with moat. What a treat to be allowed to wander through lopsided rooms, over creaking boards, up hidden stairways—undisturbed by guides and signs. Even the royal plumbing remained intact.

Pursuit of a raincoat to defy the Danish drizzles took us to a little clothing store in Faaborg. Our weather interests were diverted, happily, to something more absorbing—a recipe interview with a friendly lady clerk.

Hers is a large farm family, and in their Danish household this Apple Cake has been a Sunday winter dessert for generations. When she described it in the unfamiliar English language, she had a way of majestically understating—"When you pile whipped cream on top, this cake tastes very nice."

Though many versions of Danish apple cake are baked, this one is simply spooned into a pretty glass bowl so you can see all the layers. If you like the crumbs very crisp between layers of applesauce and jam, compile this just before serving; if you prefer a melding of ingredients, make the cake ahead of time and chill it several hours or a whole day before serving.

DANISH APPLE CAKE

1 *package* (*6-ounce size*) *zwieback, finely crushed* (*about* 2 *cups crumbs*)	1 *cup raspberry jam*
	1 *cup heavy cream*
	Sugar
6 *tablespoons melted butter*	*Vanilla*
2 *cups tart applesauce*	

Toss zwieback crumbs with melted butter. Spread ½ cup of the crumbs in bottom of glass serving bowl (about 2-quart size). Top with 1 cup of the applesauce. Make another layer of ½ cup crumbs; top with a layer of the raspberry jam. Make a third layer of ½ cup crumbs, then a layer of the remaining applesauce; top with remaining crumbs. Cover and chill, or serve immediately. At serving time, whip cream with sugar to sweeten and vanilla to flavor. Pile on top of apple cake in puffs. Spoon cake into dessert glasses or bowls to serve. *Makes 8 servings.*

Our store clerk could quote a stream of recipes. She twinkled with enthusiasm over a supper dish titled *Sammenkogt,* translated, "together cooked."

Browned chicken livers in a rich sauce of mushrooms, fresh tomatoes, and cream make a splendid dish for brunch.

CHICKEN LIVERS IN TOMATO CREAM
(*Sammenkogt*)

1 large onion, peeled and
 thinly sliced
1 pound chicken livers
½ cup (1 stick) butter
Salt
Pepper
¼ pound mushrooms, sliced

2 fresh tomatoes, peeled,
 seeded, and diced
¼ teaspoon crumbled dried
 sweet basil
1½ cups heavy cream
Crisp buttered toast points
 made from 8 slices light
 rye bread
Chopped parsley

In a frying pan, sauté onions and chicken livers in butter until onions are tender and livers are lightly brown and just cooked, about 10 minutes. Season with salt and pepper. Add mushrooms and tomatoes, and continue cooking, turning, just until mushrooms are tender. Sprinkle with sweet basil. Reduce heat, pour in cream, and simmer mixture, gently stirring occasionally, until liquid is slightly reduced, about 5 minutes. Taste sauce and correct seasoning with salt and pepper. Spoon over crisp toast points. Sprinkle each serving lightly with parsley. *Makes 6 servings.*

Bacon and eggs were never better than this: transformed into a creamy omelet, topped with big snippings of chives and bacon curls, garnished with fresh tomatoes—and titled by the Danes *Æggkage* (egg cake).

When a young housewife in Outrup introduced it to us at a country supper, she brought it to the table still hissing and sizzling in the huge hot skillet in which it was cooked. Alongside was moist, dark rye bread and butter.

EGG CAKE
(*Æggkage*)

10 *slices bacon*	*Pepper*
6 *eggs*	2 *cups milk*
3 *tablespoons flour*	2 *large tomatoes, cut in*
4 *teaspoons snipped chives*	*wedges*
Salt	

Cut 4 slices bacon in half; cut remaining slices into 2-inch pieces. In a 10-inch frying pan, cook bacon until crisp; drain on absorbent paper (roll large pieces into curls to drain). Tilt frying pan to coat all sides with bacon fat; discard excess fat. Return small bacon pieces to frying pan. Beat eggs with flour, 3 teaspoons of the chives, and salt and pepper to taste. Beat in milk. Turn into bacon-lined frying pan. Place in a moderately hot oven (375°) and bake 35 to 40 minutes or until golden and set. Sprinkle with remaining chives; garnish with bacon curls. Cut into wedges at the table and serve immediately, garnished with tomato wedges. *Makes 4 servings.*

An accommodating blond boy in the Aalborg tourist office divulged the name of the the most imaginative hostess in town—the women's editor of the local newspaper. We called at her home, and over an afternoon cup of Danish coffee, a sandwich, another sandwich, cake, and cookies, heard of the virtues of her Danish Cheese Bombe.

She likes to serve it in the evening with rye bread, crackers and glasses of beer or red wine. You might serve it for hors d'oeuvres. Turn it out of its mold onto a garnished platter bordered by a few cheese knives, so each guest can spread it on his choice of bread, crackers, or crunchy celery stalks.

This recipe responds readily to changes you might want to try—additional cheeses, paprika, mustard, green-onion seasonings. . . . One our lady editor suggested: Make the flavor "softer" by adding more whipped cream.

CHEESE BOMBE

4 ounces Camembert cheese (with crust)	*1 cup heavy cream, stiffly whipped*
4 ounces blue cheese	*¾ cup finely chopped toasted almonds*

Press softened cheeses through a fine sieve into a mixing bowl. Beat until blended and smooth. Thoroughly fold in whipped cream. Turn mixture into a lightly oiled mold (about 3 cups). Cover and chill in refrigerator 4 hours or more. At serving time, dip mold into warm water to loosen; turn cheese out onto serving platter. Very gently press almonds into top and sides of cheese. *Serves 8 generously for appetizers or evening snacks.*

From Aalborg, we journeyed southward to the lake region
surrounding Silkeborg. Summer rains brought us not the sunny
country scenery we had expected—but better yet, the first hot,
hot bath* of the trip, poufy lace-edged pillows, and a recipe for
cooking Danish boiled beef.

SILKEBORG TUB
SPLIT-LEVEL

If you would serve this boiled beef dish as the Danes do,
accompany it with buttered white bread or boiled potatoes.
Puréed vegetables thicken the sweet-sour saucing for the meat.

DANISH BOILED BEEF WITH HORSERADISH CURRANT SAUCE

4 *pounds fresh beef brisket*
or 3 pounds boneless
shoulder beef
Water
2 *teaspoons salt*
About 12 peppercorns
6 *carrots, peeled*
2 *medium-sized onions,*
peeled and cut in half

2 *stalks celery, cut in pieces*
¼ *cup dried currants*
2 *tablespoons each brown*
sugar and vinegar
½ *teaspoon prepared horse-*
radish
¼ *teaspoon each salt and*
prepared mustard

Put beef in kettle along with water to cover, salt, peppercorns,
carrots, onions, and celery. Cover kettle. Bring water to a boil;
reduce heat, and simmer 2 to 3 hours or until meat is very tender.

---

* We were intrigued by the split-level tub, though encumbered by too many
knees and elbows. Barbara was just able to squeeze her whole self into the
deeper end.

Remove meat from liquid; slice thinly; keep warm. To make sauce, strain broth, saving vegetables. Remove peppercorns from vegetables. Press vegetables through a fine strainer or whirl in a blender to make a purée. Measure 1 cup of the beef broth into a saucepan. Add vegetable purée, currants, brown sugar, vinegar, horseradish, salt, and mustard. Cook over medium heat about 5 minutes, stirring to blend. Serve beef slices with hot sauce. *Makes 8 servings.*

We expected to find fish and fish recipes at our next stop, the coastal town of Aarhus—and we did. In a country rich with excellent seafood, the plaice is probably the most exalted. It is a tender, white flatfish with a delicate flavor. In Danish, it's known as *rødspøtte* because of its bright-red skin markings. Most of the time, the Danes prefer to keep the flavor unadorned; they prepare it simply by poaching or frying.

But an inventive cook of Aarhus dreamed up this recipe to serve for special company dinners. Buttered hot French bread slices or rolls must accompany it, she says.

You don't have to have a Danish *rødspøtte* to try this recipe. Use fillet of sole or flounder, our very close counterparts.

RØDSPØTTE—
DANISH COUSIN
OF THE SOLE

FILLET OF PLAICE DE LUXE

2 packages (about 10 ounces each) chopped frozen spinach
Boiling salted water
6 tablespoons butter
4 egg yolks
½ teaspoon each salt and paprika
2 tablespoons salad oil
¼ pound Danish Tybo cheese, shredded (or use mild Cheddar cheese)
8 fillets of plaice (or sole, flounder)
Juice of 1 fresh lemon
Salt
Pepper

Cook spinach in boiling salted water just until tender; drain thoroughly. Melt butter; allow to cool slightly. Beat egg yolks thoroughly with salt and paprika. Beat in salad oil, a little at a time. Beat in melted butter, a little at a time. Stir in three fourths of the shredded cheese. Combine cheese-egg mixture with drained spinach. Pour one third of the spinach mixture in bottom of greased shallow baking dish (about 9 inches square). Season both sides of sole fillets with lemon juice, salt, and pepper. Roll up fillets and arrange each roll, loose side down, on top of spinach mixture. Pour remaining spinach over fish. Sprinkle with remaining cheese. Bake in a hot oven (400°) for 20 minutes. *Makes 8 servings.*

The same good cook found in her recipe file box her formula for a cheese soup.

Shreds of Danish cheese, melting into crunchy cubes of celery and carrots, blend to a first-course soup for a Danish (or American) dinner. Yet if you serve bigger portions, it is hearty enough for a lunch or supper main course.

A cooking note from the Aarhus recipe-benefactor: Don't let the soup boil; it might curdle if you do!

DANISH CHEESE SOUP

2 tablespoons butter	cheese (or other mild-to-
¼ cup sliced green onions	medium-sharp natural
with tops	cheese such as Cheddar,
2 tablespoons flour	Jack, Gouda)
2 cups milk	½ teaspoon salt
2 cups chicken stock	¼ teaspoon paprika
2 carrots, peeled and cut into	⅛ teaspoon pepper
¼-inch cubes	2 tablespoons freshly
⅓ cup chopped celery	chopped parsley
2 cups (about ½ pound)	Paprika
shredded Danish Danbo	

In a large saucepan, melt butter. Add onions and sauté until limp. Stir in flour, blending to make a smooth paste. Gradually add milk and stock, cooking and stirring to make a smooth, thin sauce. Add carrots, celery, cheese, salt, the ¼ teaspoon paprika, and pepper. Cover soup and simmer 15 minutes or until cheese is melted and vegetables are slightly tender; stir occasionally. Just before serving, add chopped parsley. Sprinkle top of each serving with paprika. *Makes 8 first-course or 4 main-course servings.*

Thanks to the Aarhus tourist bureau, affiliates of the nation-wide "Meet the Danes" program, we visited the home of the Deleurans. We had specified interest in meeting a good cook, and shamefully confess that we thought the evening *might* include a culinary morsel. But even our voracious appetites were unprepared for wine, five kinds of *smørrebrød*, two cakes, coffee.

Fru Deleuran's description of her recipe for Braised Stuffed Heart set off a gourmet controversy. The decision over which stuffing—prunes and apples, or parsley—is ever a debate between Fru and Herr Deleuran. Each has a preference, but they both admit either way is delicious. In any case, garnish with steamed fresh apple halves filled with currant jelly.

BRAISED STUFFED HEART

1 beef heart (about 3 pounds)	3 tablespoons shortening
Salt	1 medium-sized onion, peeled and chopped
Pepper	2 tablespoons water (or more)
⅓ cup pieces of cut dried prunes	3 cooking apples
½ cooking apple, peeled and chopped	2 tablespoons red currant jelly

Wash heart; trim away hard parts and any outer membrane. Sprinkle heart cavity and outside with salt and pepper to taste. Combine cut prunes and chopped apple and press into heart cavity. Close opening with skewers. In a heavy pan, brown heart on all sides in 2 tablespoons of the shortening. Remove heart from pan; add remaining shortening and onion. Sauté onion until limp. Return heart to pan; add water. Cover and simmer heart 1½ hours or until tender (add more water during cooking period if necessary). Peel, halve, and core apples; place in pan with heart. Cover pan and simmer 15 minutes more or until apples are tender. Remove heart and apples to serving platter; keep warm. Press onions and remaining pan drippings through a fine strainer (or whirl in a blender). Heat, taste and correct seasoning, (add water if too thick), and serve as meat sauce. Fill each apple half with a spoonful of jelly. Remove skewers from heart. Cut heart, across the grain, into thick slices to serve. *Makes 6 servings.*

Variation: Follow directions above, but stuff heart cavity very tightly with fresh parsley sprigs.

One of the cakes Mrs. Deleuran made for our sampling was *Brunsviger.** On the island of Funen, where it originated, the bakers make this cake from a sweet yeast dough that has risen as far as it will go—and a thin top crusting of caramelized brown sugar.

---

* Sausage-lovers be warned: don't confuse this with *Braunschweiger.*

Mrs. Deleuran says it's a lot more fun to make—and tastes better—if, as it bakes, you punch dimples in the dough whenever it begins to ascend. That way, you get much more of the crunchy sugar topping in proportion to the base.

BROWN-SUGARED COFFEE CAKE
(*Brunsviger*)

1 package yeast (active dry or compressed)	3 tablespoons butter
	3 tablespoons sugar
¼ cup water (warm for dry yeast, lukewarm for compressed)	½ teaspoon salt
	½ teaspoon ground or finely crushed cardamom
½ cup milk	1½ cups all-purpose flour

Topping:

¼ cup (½ stick) butter, melted
½ cup brown sugar, firmly packed
1 tablespoon light or dark corn syrup

Sprinkle yeast into water; stir to dissolve. Scald milk; pour over butter, sugar, and salt in a large mixing bowl. Stir until butter is melted and milk has cooled to lukewarm. Stir in dissolved yeast and cardamom. Sift flour, measure, add to milk mixture. Stir to mix thoroughly. Cover bowl and allow dough to rise in a warm place for about 20 minutes. Stir dough to remove air bubbles.

Spread in an 8- or 9-inch square greased baking pan. Stir together melted butter, brown sugar, and corn syrup. Drizzle spoonfuls of mixture over top of dough as evenly as possible. Bake in a very hot oven (450°) for 25 to 30 minutes or until dough is golden brown and topping is bubbly and caramelized. (About three times during baking, gently punch dough down in several places with the handle of a wooden spoon.) Allow to cool slightly. Cut into strips and serve warm. *Makes about 12 pieces.*

Before leaving the Deleurans', we were allowed two special treats—a peek at the sleeping blond children, a view of the neighbor's rooftop stork's nest.

Luckily, our route back to Copenhagen took us through the heart of the dairy country, Fuglebjerg, and to the Jensens' modern home and creamery. Mr. and Mrs. Jensen are a warm-hearted pair with a talent for making foreign guests feel at home. Moments after our arrival, we were shelling peas in the kitchen, prowling around the dairy, sniffing the rows of aging cheeses.

As we were leaving the garden, the swift-moving Mrs. Jensen swooped down and broke off the tender heart of a head of palest green butter lettuce.

It would never be right to burden the subtle sweetness of that garden lettuce with anything but the lightest dressing of cream and sugar and a suspicion of mild vinegar.

CREAM AND SUGAR LETTUCE SALAD

1 head very tender butter let-   *3 tablespoons white cider*
*   tuce, washed and thor-*   *   vinegar*
*   oughly drained and dried*   *2 tablespoons sugar*
¼ cup heavy cream

Break lettuce leaves into salad bowl. Stir together thoroughly cream, vinegar, and sugar. Pour cream dressing over lettuce and toss gently. *Makes 4 servings.*

It was at the Jensens' dairy that we tasted the best dessert of our lives.

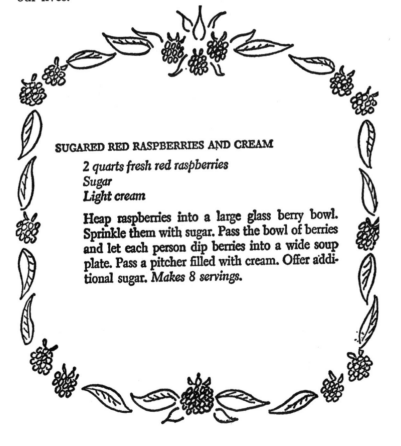

SUGARED RED RASPBERRIES AND CREAM

2 quarts fresh red raspberries
Sugar
Light cream

Heap raspberries into a large glass berry bowl. Sprinkle them with sugar. Pass the bowl of berries and let each person dip berries into a wide soup plate. Pass a pitcher filled with cream. Offer additional sugar. *Makes 8 servings.*

Too many portions of an expansive Danish noontime dinner produced an unconcealable drowse. Mrs. Jensen led us into the living room, turned on soft music, and insisted that we put our feet up for the traditional post-dinner nap. We awakened to the music of clinking silverware and prospects of afternoon coffee.

Soon we were trying out a cake-like spice bread. Mrs. Jensen makes it often. When warm and freshly baked, she cuts it into big cubes and tops each with a spoonful of sour cream for dinner dessert. The next day, when it's cool and easy to slice, she offers buttered thin strips of it on the afternoon-coffee tray.

SPICECAKE LOAF
(*Krydderikage*)

½ cup (1 stick) butter or margarine
1½ cups brown sugar, firmly packed
2 eggs
2¾ cups flour
1½ teaspoons baking powder
1 to 1½ teaspoons ground or finely crushed cardamom
1½ teaspoons cinnamon
⅛ teaspoon salt
⅓ cup cream
⅓ cup dried currants

In a large mixing bowl, beat butter until soft and creamy. Gradually add sugar and beat until creamy. Beat in eggs, one at a time. Sift flour, measure, and sift again with baking powder, cardamom, cinnamon, and salt. Add sifted dry ingredients to creamed mixture alternately with the cream, beginning and ending with dry ingredients; mix well after each addition. Stir in currants. Turn batter into a greased 5- by 9-inch loaf pan. Bake in a moderate oven (350°) for 50 minutes or until toothpick inserted in center comes out clean. Serve either warm or cool. *Makes about 10 dessert servings or 24 slices coffee bread.*

We praised Mrs. Jensen's chewy macaroons, and learned another cooking secret. According to her, there's no point in making coconut macaroons with only the whites of the eggs when cookies are yellower, softer, and better-tasting when you use whole eggs. (Perhaps her cookies have an added advantage —they're made with big fresh eggs, just laid by the Jensen chickens!)

GOLDEN COCONUT MACAROONS

2 eggs	1 package (8 ounces)
⅔ cup sugar	shredded coconut (about
½ teaspoon almond extract	2 cups)

Beat eggs slightly in a mixing bowl. Add sugar, almond extract and coconut; stir to mix thoroughly. Drop mixture by heaping teaspoonfuls onto a well-greased baking sheet. Bake in a moderate oven (350°) for 12 minutes or until cookies are lightly browned. Remove to a wire rack to cool. *Makes about 3 dozen.*

Expressing a fear that our unrestrained appetites might soon make it difficult for us to squeeze into our small car, Mrs. Jensen consoled us: "Volkswagens have big front doors."

We turned toward Copenhagen, delirious with thoughts of that fabled city. We had been saving it for last.

Our first day was packed with memorable sights:

Elderly women by the canal stripping skin off eels and deftly discarding fish heads.

Everyone blond and rosy-cheeked.

Beehive ("Candy Floss") hairdos and crisp, pleated white skirts.

Bicyclers of all shapes and sizes, carrying flowers, brief-cases, books, lunch packets.

A basement cheese shop, a parcel string-tied with a wooden handle.

Lodging at the home of Fru Andersen provided some un-hinging moments. As Barbara gathered courage to step into a frigid bath one evening, a young man bolted through the door.

When we inquired about the lock first thing next morning, we were given a priceless demonstration: hurl full weight against door, twist key at moment of impact. (If one values privacy, athletic skill and split-second timing are imperative!)

Fru Andersen had some thoughts on cookery well worth sharing.

Danish families, she said, often anticipate the leftovers as much as the original roast. Upcoming is a supper of *Bikse-mad*—a grandly glorified hash. She adds fried apple slices to the usual recipe.

DANISH HASH
(*Biksemad*)

About ¼ cup butter	½ apple (unpeeled), cored
¼ pound roast or boiled	and sliced into rings
beef, pork, or veal, cut	Salt
into ½-inch cubes	Pepper
¼ cup diced cooked potatoes	1 egg
1 small onion, peeled and	Dill pickle
thinly sliced	Worcestershire sauce
	Catsup

Brown well on all sides in butter, each ingredient separately, the meat, potatoes, onion, and apple. Season each browned item with salt and pepper. Arrange on warm serving plate in layers—first meat, then potatoes, then onions, then overlapping apple rings. Fry egg in butter and place on top. Garnish plate with a dill pickle; pass Worcestershire and catsup. *Makes 1 serving.*

Fru Andersen garnishes a platter of beef rolls with fresh parsley sprigs and bacon cooked until almost crisp, then curled.

COPENHAGEN PARSLEY BEEF ROLL-UPS

1½ pounds sliced beef	Parsley sprigs
round, pounded very thin	Flour
Salt	¼ cup butter
Pepper	1½ cups milk
2 tablespoons instant minced	2 teaspoons flour
onions	1 tablespoon water
8 four-inch strips bacon	1 teaspoon soy sauce

Cut meat into 8 pieces. Sprinkle one side of each meat slice with salt and pepper to taste and minced onions. Place a bacon strip and fresh parsley sprig in center. Roll up and fasten with a toothpick. Dust with flour. Over medium heat, brown rolls on all sides in butter. Pour in milk, cover, and simmer about 1½ hours or until meat is tender. Just before serving, remove rolls to warm serving dish. Remove toothpicks. Mix to a smooth paste the flour and the water. Gradually beat paste into simmering liquid. Add soy sauce. Continue to heat and stir until liquid is thickened and flavors blended, about 4 minutes. Correct gravy seasoning with salt and pepper. Pour part of gravy over beef rolls; pass the remainder. *Makes 4 servings.*

Refreshing with the whiff of lemon, Fru Andersen's luncheon salad is elegant and hearty.

SMOKED SALMON
LUNCHEON SALAD BOWL

½ cup salad oil
¼ cup fresh lemon juice
½ teaspoon each salt and pepper
2 medium-sized potatoes, peeled, cooked, chilled, and sliced
1 head romaine, washed, drained and dried

¼ pound fresh mushrooms, sliced
6 to 8 ounces smoked salmon, cut in slivers
4 hard-cooked eggs, sliced
½ to 1 teaspoon dried dill weed

Shake together salad oil, lemon juice, salt, and pepper to make dressing. Pour over potato slices; allow to stand 10 minutes. Break romaine into large chilled salad bowl. Drain dressing from potatoes and save. Arrange in a pattern over top of romaine the drained sliced potatoes, mushrooms, smoked salmon, and eggs. Sprinkle with dill weed. Just before serving, toss at table with reserved dressing. Lift salad into chilled individual salad bowls to serve. *Makes 6 luncheon salad servings.*

Early in our stay in Copenhagen, we met Karen, the writer of a Danish cookbook for Danish cooks. From the first an enthusiastic supporter of our cookbook cause, she steered us to many good foods and concocted some of her own selections for us to sample. On one occasion, she invited us to join a group of her affable relatives for dinner at her house.

To open the meal, Karen served *gravad* (buried) fresh salmon on buttered white toast.

When you serve it, thinly slice the dill-sprinkled red salmon, and arrange it on a small platter. Let each guest help himself to a slice of buttered bread or toast, and top it with salmon. Eat with knife and fork as an appetizer *smørrebrød* or, in miniature version, as a finger-food hors d'oeuvre.

GRAVAD SALMON

1 pound filleted fresh red salmon	⅛ teaspoon coarsely ground black pepper
2 tablespoons salt	4 teaspoons dried dill weed
1½ tablespoons sugar	Buttered white bread or toast

Divide salmon into 2 pieces. Mix salt, sugar, pepper, and 2 teaspoons of the dill. Sprinkle evenly over one side of one of the salmon pieces. Top with second piece of salmon. Sprinkle remaining dill over top of second salmon piece. Cover salmon with a plate; place a weight on the plate. Chill in refrigerator for 12 to 24 hours. Just before serving, cut salmon into thin slices. Serve with bread or toast slices. *Makes 12 appetizer servings.*

It was Danish Karen who first introduced us to *Swedish* meatballs. The touch of the artist in this recipe is the addition of a
bit of liver to give an elusive nutty flavor.

SWEDISH MEATBALLS WITH MUSHROOMS AND
SOUR CREAM GRAVY

¾ *pound lean beef*
¼ *pound fat pork meat*
2 *ounces baby beef liver*
¼ *cup fine dry bread crumbs*
½ *cup milk*
1 *egg, beaten*
1 *small onion, minced*
1 *tablespoon finely chopped fresh parsley*
½ *teaspoon salt*

¼ *teaspoon pepper*
⅛ *teaspoon each crumbled dried basil, marjoram, rose-mary, and thyme*
About ¼ *cup butter*
6 *ounces fresh mushrooms, sliced*
Sour Cream Sauce (recipe below)

Have your meat man grind together the beef, pork, and
liver once (or grind it yourself, using medium-sized plate on meat
grinder). Soak bread crumbs in milk. Mix together thoroughly
with the beef, pork, liver, egg, onion, parsley, salt, pepper, and
herbs. Working with wet hands, form meat mixture into balls
about 1 inch in diameter. Over medium heat, melt butter in a
large frying pan. Add meatballs and brown on all sides, shaking
the pan to turn balls and keep them rounded. Remove meatballs
from frying pan; turn into baking dish with cover (about 1½-
quart size). Add mushrooms to frying pan and sauté until tender
(add more butter to frying pan if necessary). Turn mushrooms
over meatballs. Pour Sour Cream Sauce over meatballs and mushrooms. Cover dish and bake in a moderate oven (350°) for 20
minutes. *Makes 6 servings.*

Sour Cream Sauce: Loosen drippings from bottom of frying pan.
Stir in ¼ cup water, 2 teaspoons soy sauce, ⅛ teaspoon pepper,
and 1/16 teaspoon *each* crumbled dried basil, marjoram, rosemary,
and thyme. Reduce heat, stir in 1 cup commercial sour cream.
Heat and stir until smooth.

KAREN'S CARROTS

1 medium-sized onion, thinly
    sliced
6 tablespoons butter
4 large carrots, peeled and

very thinly sliced
½ teaspoon salt
¼ teaspoon curry powder
⅛ teaspoon pepper

In a frying pan with cover, sauté onion in 2 tablespoons of the butter until limp. Add carrots, salt, curry powder, pepper, and remaining butter. Cover and cook over moderate heat, stirring occasionally, 15 minutes or until carrots are just tender. *Makes 4 servings.*

Karen's family lived on a small Danish farm when she was growing up. For a summertime supper this was a favorite dish —made from vine-ripened red tomatoes and green beans plucked from the garden.

PEPPERED GREEN BEANS
WITH PORK

1½ pounds whole fresh green
    beans (or 2 packages, 9
    ounces each, frozen green
    beans)
⅔ pound fresh tomatoes,
    peeled and seeded
¼ pound salt pork, cut into
    thin strips

4 tablespoons water
2 tablespoons butter
1 teaspoon freshly ground
    black pepper
Salt

In a large pan with cover, combine beans, tomatoes, salt pork, water, butter, and pepper. Cover and simmer 1 hour or until beans are very tender; stir occasionally. Taste and add salt if necessary. *Makes 8 servings.*

Sweet caramelized onions are traditional garnish for a Danish rare roast beef. Karen's have a touch of rosemary.

HERB GLAZED ONIONS

2 pounds small boiling onions, peeled
Boiling salted water
3 tablespoons butter

6 tablespoons brown sugar
⅛ to ¼ teaspoon crumbled dried rosemary

Add onions to boiling salted water. Cook in gently boiling water 10 minutes or until almost tender. Drain onions and dry on absorbent paper towels. In a large heavy frying pan, slowly melt butter with brown sugar. Cook over low heat, stirring to mix. Add onions and turn them in the syrup until almost all the syrup clings to onions and they are tender, about 15 minutes. During last few minutes of cooking, sprinkle with rosemary. *Makes 6 servings.*

This tangy fruit topping goes with almost any fruit. Karen suggests it for chilled fresh apricots or sliced bananas with red cherries.

Dark crumbs of pumpernickel or rye bread crisp-fry in butter. You sweeten them with raw sugar or brown sugar, and sprinkle the mixture thickly over creamy yogurt.

YOGURT (OR SOUR CREAM)—CRUMB FRUIT TOPPING

½ cup fine soft dark pumper-
nickel or rye-bread crumbs
1 tablespoon butter

2 tablespoons (or more) raw
sugar or brown sugar
1 cup chilled plain yogurt (or
sour cream)

Slowly sauté bread crumbs in butter until toasted and very crisp, stirring frequently. Allow crumbs to cool and drain on absorbent paper. Mix with sugar to sweeten. Whip yogurt until smooth; turn into serving bowl; sprinkle with crumb mixture. Spoon over chilled fruits. *Makes topping for 4 fruit servings.*

We asked the bashful young Dane if he spoke English. Honest reply: "Oh, a small."

Sight-seeing in Copenhagen is a slow process when one is constantly sidetracked by tempting pastry windows and enticing aromas.

Attending a church service one morning, expanded shapes conspicuously wedged into the front pew—we felt chagrin. The very British minister had chosen "fahsting" as his sermon topic!

There's one miraculous baker's treat that gladdened our taste travels throughout Denmark—butter cake! It's a feat most Danish homemakers leave to their baker. But once back at home, we couldn't resist an attempt to re-create it—so you might share our rapture, and so we could have another taste ourselves!

Every bite tastes like the best part because of all the "*snav*" (the Danes' coined term for the oozing rich butter-and-sugar filling).

DANISH BUTTER CAKE

½ cup (1 stick) butter
2 tablespoons flour
3 tablespoons sugar
¾ cup milk, scalded
1 package yeast (active dry or compressed)
3 tablespoons water (warm for dry yeast, lukewarm for compressed)
1 egg, slightly beaten

2½ cups flour
¾ teaspoon salt
Pastry Filling (recipe below)
Pastry Cream (recipe below)
2 tablespoons raisins
1 egg white, beaten
3 tablespoons slivered almonds
Orange Icing (recipe below)

Using a pastry blender or two knives, cut the ½ cup butter into the 2 tablespoons flour. Gather into a ball. Flatten out into a 7-inch square on a baking sheet. Place in freezer for 20 minutes. Stir the 3 tablespoons sugar into scalded milk; cool to lukewarm. Sprinkle or crumble yeast into water; stir to dissolve. Combine egg and yeast mixture with lukewarm milk. Sift flour, measure, and sift again with salt into large mixing bowl. Add yeast mixture; beat until smooth. Turn dough onto a floured board and roll into a rectangle 7 by 14 inches. Loosen butter mixture from baking sheet with a spatula; lift onto one half of the rectangle. Fold remaining half of dough rectangle over butter; roll out. Fold over one third of the dough from the left, then one third from the right (as for a letter), and roll out. Repeat folding of both sides of dough twice more. Chill dough in refrigerator 30 minutes. Cut off one third of the dough (return remainder to refrigerator), and roll out to a circle 10 inches in diameter. Place in a greased 9-inch springform pan to line bottom of pan and form a ½-inch edge up the side of pan. Roll out remaining dough into a rectangle about 9 by 12 inches. Spread evenly, almost to edges, with Pastry Filling. Spread half of the Pastry Cream over Filling. Sprinkle with raisins. Starting with long side, roll up as for jelly roll. Spread remaining Pastry Cream over dough lining springform pan. With a sharp knife, cut roll into 10 slices. Place one slice, cut side up, in center of pan. Arrange remaining slices around center slice to fill pan. Gently brush tops with beaten egg white. Sprinkle with almonds. Allow to rise in a warm place 40 minutes or until light. Bake in a moderately hot oven (375°) for 35 minutes or until golden brown. Remove to wire rack to cool. While warm, drizzle Orange Icing over top. Allow to cool partially before cutting. Slice into wedges to serve. *Makes 12 servings.*

Pastry Filling: Cream together thoroughly ½ cup (1 stick) soft butter, ½ cup sugar, and ½ teaspoon vanilla.

Pastry Cream: Scald ¾ cup milk. In top of double boiler, beat together with a spoon 2 egg yolks and ¼ cup sugar until creamy. Add 2 tablespoons flour, a few grains of salt, and ½ teaspoon vanilla, stirring just to blend. Gradually beat in hot milk. Place over hot water and cook, stirring vigorously, until mixture reaches boiling point (do not let it boil). Strain through a fine sieve. Allow to cool; stir occasionally.

Orange Icing: Stir together ½ cup sifted powdered sugar, ½ teaspoon grated orange peel, and 2 teaspoons orange juice.

We couldn't resist a final binge at our most cherished Copenhagen pastry shop, an indulgence that almost caused us to miss the ferry to Sweden. Two handsome policemen at the docks noted our frenzy, stopped traffic, and personally escorted us, our car, and our bulging pastry sacks aboard a boat bound for Malmö.

SAVORING SWEDEN

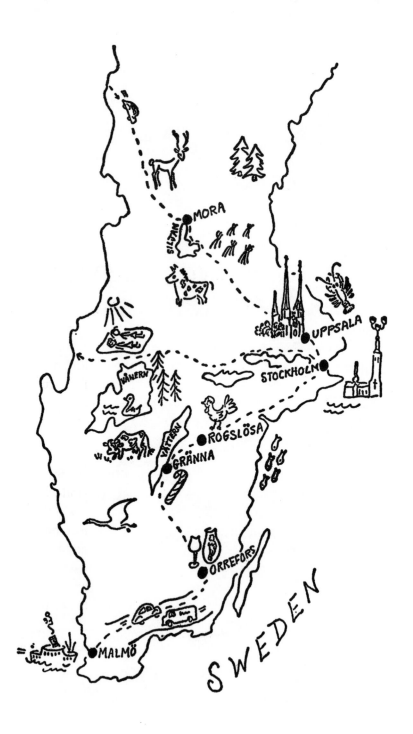

Our first nonedible objective in Sweden was the Orrefors crystal factory, found hidden in the forests along an obscure dirt road. The factory furnace room provided one of life's greatest textural thrills: burly men dashing about with pokers, stabbing and swirling them in the hot, molten crystal mixture, blowing and twirling and sometimes plunging them into molds, snipping off blobs with scissors and letting them fall into round spinning bowls.

On to Lake Vättern and Gränna, a town famous for its homemade *"Polkagrisar"* (polka pigs)—fat red-and-white striped peppermint candy sticks.

Fru Bergman, the industrious manager of a tourist hotel, told us how to combat a cold winter's night in Scandinavia: Invite friends in about eight o'clock and serve an open shrimp omelet and glasses of dry red wine. Set the omelet before your company while it still bubbles in the pan—with many tiny shrimp reclining on the top—and cut it into fat quarter-circle pieces. (She would offer, too, a trayful of thin-sliced dark-bread rounds, unsalted butter crackers, and two or three kinds of cheese. Later, cakes and coffee.)

OPEN SHRIMP OMELET

6 *eggs*	¼ *cup butter*
6 *tablespoons heavy cream*	1 *cup tiny cooked shrimp*
½ *teaspoon salt*	*Dried dill weed*
⅛ *teaspoon pepper*	

Beat eggs with cream, salt, and pepper until thoroughly blended. Heat 2 tablespoons of the butter in large omelet pan or frying pan (10 to 11 inches in diameter) until it bubbles. Pour in egg mixture. Cook as a French omelet, lifting and tilting pan to let the uncooked egg flow to bottom of pan; do not fold. Meanwhile, melt remaining butter, add shrimp, and toss to coat with butter. Sprinkle shrimp over top of cooked omelet. Slip under broiler for a few moments—just to heat shrimp. Lightly sprinkle dill weed over top of omelet. Cut into quarters and serve immediately. *Makes 4 servings.*

With a pause to pick wild raspberries along the way, we continued north from Gränna. A picnic lunch in a Swedish farm meadow near Roglösa led to . . . an afternoon snooze in the sun . . . led to . . . making friends with Marget and Stefan, the young couple who own the farm . . . led to . . . an over-night stay on the farm (including gathering eggs and meeting roosters with floppy combs) . . . led to . . . an account of some of Marget's best recipes.

Swedes love Jensen's Temptation—with anchovy seasoning. We like it better—with smoked sausages.

JENSEN'S TEMPTATION

2 large onions, chopped	8 flat canned anchovy fillets,
¼ cup butter	drained (or 2 to 4 link
3 medium-sized potatoes,	smoked sausages, thinly
peeled and thinly sliced	sliced crosswise)
Salt	About 1 cup milk or cream
Pepper	1 cup shredded cheese

Sauté onions in butter until limp. Arrange one third of the potatoes over bottom of a greased baking dish (about 1½ quart). Sprinkle with salt and pepper to taste. Spread half the sautéed onions over potatoes; top with 4 anchovy fillets (or half the sliced sausages). Repeat layers of potatoes (season with salt and pepper),

onions, and anchovies or sausages. Top with remaining one third
of the potatoes (season). Pour milk (enough to reach within
¾ inch of top of potatoes) over potatoes. Sprinkle with cheese.
Bake in a moderate oven (350°) for 1 hour or until potatoes are
tender. Slip under broiler to brown cheese, if you wish. *Makes
4 to 6 servings.*

Not for everyday fare are these marinated tomatoes, Marget
admonished, but for a party meal or a *smörgåsbord* table.

SMÖRGÅSBORD TOMATOES

6 *small-to medium-sized*
  tomatoes
Boiling water
1 *clove garlic*
1 *cup salad oil*
⅓ *cup wine vinegar*

¾ *teaspoon each salt and*
  pepper
⅛ *teaspoon sugar*
¼ *cup snipped chives*
Crisp salad greens

Dip tomatoes in boiling water for a few moments to loosen
skins; peel and remove cores. Slice each tomato in half and remove as much of the seedy portion as possible. Rub the inside of
a salad bowl with split clove of garlic. With the cut sides down,
place tomatoes in salad bowl. Shake together thoroughly the oil,
vinegar, salt, pepper, sugar, and all but about 2 teaspoons of the
chives. Pour dressing over tomatoes. Cover salad bowl and chill
tomatoes in refrigerator at least 2 hours. Just before serving,
spoon dressing over tomatoes and sprinkle with remaining chives.
Garnish with a border of crisp salad greens. *Makes 6 servings.*

In the summertime, Stefan and Marget catch perch in the lake behind their country farmhouse. Then Marget fries them for a summer supper this way—so the sandwiched fillets are crunchy and golden on the outside, moist and juicy in the middle.

PERCH FILLETS LAYERED WITH CHIVES

1½ *pounds perch fillets*	2 *eggs, beaten*
Salt	*About 2 cups crushed potato*
Pepper	*chips*
About 2 tablespoons snipped	6 *tablespoons butter*
fresh chives	*Lemon slices*

Sprinkle fillets on both sides with salt and pepper to taste. Sprinkle snipped chives evenly over one side of half of the fillets. Top each chive-covered fillet with another, sandwich-fashion. Handling carefully, dip "sandwiches" into beaten egg, then into crumbs. (If you have trouble handling fillet sandwiches, pin each together with 2 toothpicks; remove before serving.) Melt butter in a large frying pan until it bubbles. Add fish and sauté over medium heat until golden brown and crisp on the outside, flaky at the center, about 6 minutes on each side. Turn only once. Serve immediately with slices of lemon. *Makes 6 servings.*

Ready for a more urban life, we approached Stockholm.

We promptly settled down in the home of the Thors, in a hexagonal-shaped room with one balcony, one Siamese cat (live!), two crystal chandeliers, and thirty-two paintings. (Herr Thor is an artist, though not destined to become one of the great masters.)

Fru Thor, the obvious administrator of the household, told us of three wonderful ways with lamb.

WINE-BAKED LAMB
SHANKS WITH DILL GRAPES

4 lamb shanks	Flour
Water	Salt
Celery tops	Pepper
1 clove garlic, peeled and split	1 cup dry red wine
1 bay leaf	¼ cup salad oil
10 peppercorns	Brown meat coloring
1 teaspoon salt	1 tablespoon dry red wine
¼ teaspoon dried dill weed	Dill Grapes (recipe below)

Place lamb shanks in large kettle with cover. Add water just to cover. Add celery tops, garlic, bay leaf, peppercorns, salt, and dill weed. Cover and simmer 1 hour. Remove shanks from broth. Strain broth; skim off excess fat. Dust shanks with flour seasoned with salt and pepper. Arrange in single layer in greased baking pan. Combine wine and oil and pour evenly over lamb. Bake in a moderately hot oven (375°) for 1 hour or until shanks are crisp and brown (turn once and baste frequently during baking). Remove shanks to serving platter; keep warm. Discard excess fat from drippings. Make gravy from drippings in pan and strained broth: thicken with flour; add brown meat coloring to color gravy; just before serving stir in 1 tablespoon red wine. Offer gravy to ladle over meat. Accompany shanks with Dill Grapes. *Makes 4 servings.*

Dill Grapes: In a small frying pan, melt 2 tablespoons butter. Add 2 cups seedless white grapes (or halved and seeded red grapes) and a pinch of dried dill weed. Sprinkle with 1 teaspoon sugar. Sauté grapes, gently stirring, just until heated through.

ROAST LAMB WITH CUCUMBER HOLLANDAISE

1 leg of lamb, 5 to 6 pounds	1 tablespoon lemon juice
Salt	¼ teaspoon salt
Pepper	⅛ teaspoon cayenne
Dill weed	¼ cup hot water
½ cup (1 stick) butter, melted	2 cucumbers, peeled
	Boiling salted water
2 eggs, beaten	Lemon slices

Rub surface of lamb with salt and pepper and dill weed. Roast as usual, basting occasionally with drippings.

Before serving time, make Hollandaise sauce (or use 1 can, 6 ounces, Hollandaise sauce, heat in top of double boiler over hot water, and add a dash of dill weed): Slowly add melted butter to beaten eggs, beating constantly with a wire whip. Turn butter-egg mixture into top of double boiler; cook, stirring, over hot (not boiling) water until thickened. Add lemon juice, salt, cayenne, hot water, and a dash of dill weed; stir until blended.

Slice cucumbers in quarters, lengthwise; slice thinly crosswise. Cook cucumbers in a small amount of boiling salted water just until tender. Drain thoroughly, and fold into hot hollandaise sauce. Place roast lamb on carving platter; garnish with lemon slices. Slice lamb and serve with sauce. *Makes about 8 servings.*

COFFEE-BASTED ROAST LAMB

1 leg of lamb, 5 to 6 pounds	
Salt	2 tablespoons sugar
Pepper	Flour
1 cup hot, strong coffee	Water
¼ cup light cream	Red currant jelly

Rub surface of lamb with salt and pepper. Roast as usual. Baste during last hour of roasting with coffee mixed with cream and sugar. Make gravy from pan drippings: Skim off excess fat; thicken with flour; use water for additional liquid. Add salt and pepper to taste. Stir into gravy 1 tablespoon currant jelly for each cup of liquid; heat and stir until melted. Serve gravy with lamb. *Makes about 8 servings.*

Stockholm specialties:

Mothers browsing in shops—their baby carriages left unguarded on the streets.

A ticket saleslady unobtrusively scotch-taping our battered map while discussing opera seats.

Splashing in rain puddles, huddled under a voluminous raincoat and hood, eating a banana.

Frantic to find an opera festival said to be in a Stockholm suburb, we barged into the office of THE POLIZEI to get directions. A routine case? Three sober-faced policemen immediately went into action, as though tracking down a criminal—flipping through files, putting through urgent phone calls. Finally the verdict, "No opera this week."

A hair-raising ride into the unknown aboard the Stockholm subway shot us to the home of Mr. Hallen, an aging bachelor with a passion for flowers, 1880 wine, and gourmet cooking. (The "Sweden at Home" program, a liaison between foreign visitors and Swedish citizens of similar interests, arranged the evening.)

After a few sips of wine and some cordial conversation, our sociable host launched into a description of three dinner-party recipes.

He has a knack for streamlining preparations to absolute minimum effort. As he says, this fish dish is "very comfortable to make." Use the same baking dish for marinating, baking, and serving the fish. (If you're in a hurry, you don't *have* to marinate it.)

BAKED WHITEFISH IN PARSLEY SAUCE

2 pounds fillets of any white-
fish (or use fish steaks
about ½-inch thick)
⅔ cup melted butter
½ cup chopped fresh parsley

1½ to 2 tablespoons lemon
juice
½ teaspoon each salt and
pepper

Arrange fish in single layer on bottom of shallow baking dish. Combine butter, parsley, lemon juice, salt, and pepper; pour over fish. Allow fish to marinate 30 minutes. Bake in a moderate oven (350°) for 10 to 20 minutes or until fish flakes easily when tested with a fork. *Makes 6 servings.*

With twelve hours' marinating in nutty sherry wine and slow baking in rich cream, rolled slices of Swedish ham emerge with a smooth flavor. Mr. Hallen's accompaniment suggestion: inch-thick sticks of light rye bread with caraway, generously brushed with melted butter and toasted crisp in the oven.

SHERRIED HAM IN CREAM

> 12 thin slices baked or boiled ham (about 1½ pounds meat)
> 1 cup dry sherry
> 1½ cups heavy cream
> 1½ cups shredded Edam or Gouda cheese

Marinate ham in sherry in refrigerator for 12 hours; turn ham occasionally. Remove ham from sherry; roll. Arrange rolls in a single layer in a greased shallow baking dish, placing loose ends down. Pour cream over ham. Sprinkle cheese evenly over top. Bake in a moderate oven (350°) for 30 minutes. *Makes 6 servings.*

A flamboyant dessert is the only proper climax to a formal dinner graciously executed by Mr. Hallen. He carries international cuisine almost to the limit, juxtaposing Chinese baked bananas, French brandy flambé, and Italian zabaglione.

FLAMING BANANAS WITH ORANGE ZABAGLIONE

4 egg yolks   *¼ teaspoon vanilla*
¼ cup sugar   *6 ripe but firm bananas*
¼ teaspoon salt   *⅓ cup warm brandy*
6 tablespoons orange juice

Make zabaglione: In a small mixing bowl, beat egg yolks until thick and lemon-colored. Beat in sugar, salt, orange juice, and vanilla. Turn into top part of double boiler. Cook over hot water, beating constantly, until thickened (about 5 minutes).

Place unpeeled bananas in a single layer on greased heat-proof serving platter. Bake in a very hot oven (450°) for 10 minutes or until peels are black. Working quickly with knife and fork (the bananas *must* be served hot!), remove peels from bananas. Light heated brandy in a ladle, and pour, flaming, over bananas. Baste flaming brandy over bananas until flame dies. To serve, gently lift bananas onto individual warm dessert plates. Pass warm zabaglione for guests to spoon onto hot bananas. *Makes 6 servings.*

Our suitcases were already beginning to rebel against shopping sprees, but who could resist place mats decorated with bold striped pigs—or red velvet mice—or handwoven fabrics? At least we managed to keep our currency puzzlements to ourselves (avoiding a phrase used by one young American tourist: "How much is it in real money?").

A Swedish suit—a thing of glory.

Alterations—mandatory!

Hard to keep a poised exterior,
When standing before a three-way
mirror watching an amused
tailor make chalk
marks down one's
posterior.

On a second occasion, the "Sweden at Home" program came to our aid and directed us to an accomplished hostess, Mrs. Ekberg. At the slightest excuse, she will drop everything and give a party in her antique-furnished city apartment. Her recipe repertoire is enormous.

Almost as important to the design of a Swedish company dinner as the indispensable dessert is a tasty "entrance" to the meal. In the summer, Mrs. Ekberg arranges a buffet platter or individual first-course plates with a seafood salad. She insists that you prepare it at the last minute so every ingredient will be very cold, and the lettuce crisp.

SEAFOOD-SALAD APPETIZER PLATTER

18 *large shrimp, peeled and*   ¾ *cup cooked, chilled green*
cleaned   *peas*
Boiling salted water   6 *tablespoons mayonnaise*
1 *head butter lettuce, rinsed*   2 *tomatoes, peeled, chilled,*
and well drained   *and cut into thin wedges*
1 *cup flaked crab meat*   *Lemon wedges*
                                         Buttered white-bread toast

Drop shrimp into boiling salted water; bring water to a boil again, then simmer until shrimp turn color, about 10 minutes. Drain shrimp; chill thoroughly. At serving time, cut lettuce into very thin strips and arrange in a bed on a chilled platter (or individual plates). Arrange crab meat over lettuce, leaving a border of lettuce. Sprinkle peas over crab. Spread mayonnaise in a thin coating over crab and peas. Arrange shrimp decoratively on top of mayonnaise. Garnish platter (or plates) with tomato and lemon wedges. Serve with small slices of buttered white-bread toast. *Makes 6 servings.*

At a winter dinner at Mrs. Ekberg's, a tiny hot cheese pastry often appears beside a first-course cup of steaming bouillon.

Use bits of any three cheeses you like, but it is best to seek one pungent, one creamy, one firm and mild.

HOT CHEESE TARTS

1 cup flour	1 ounce crumbled blue
¼ teaspoon salt	cheese
6 tablespoons butter	2 ounces softened cream
About ¼ cup heavy cream	cheese
1 egg	½ cup shredded Cheddar
1 tablespoon heavy cream	cheese
	Cayenne

Sift flour with salt into mixing bowl. With pastry blender or two knives, cut butter into flour until particles are the size of small peas. Add just enough cream to form a soft dough, tossing lightly with a fork to mix. On a lightly floured board, roll out dough very thin (less than ⅛ inch). Line tart pans with pastry, overlapping sides of pans slightly (to prevent sides from slipping to center of pans during baking). Prick bottom and sides of tart shells with a floured fork. Bake in a hot oven (425°) for 10 minutes or until golden brown. Allow shells to cool in pans for a few moments; gently remove to wire racks. Meantime beat egg with cream. Add cheeses and mix thoroughly. Place tart shells on baking sheet. Gently spoon cheese mixture into shells. Sprinkle with cayenne. Bake in a moderate oven (350°) about 10 minutes or until cheese is puffed and set. Serve at once. *Makes about 12 appetizer tarts.*

Mrs. Ekberg dresses poached whitefish with a buttery dill sauce, thickened solely with fine dices of hard-cooked eggs.

POACHED WHITEFISH WITH LEMON EGG SAUCE

1½ *pounds whitefish fillets*	6 *tablespoons butter*
or steaks	1 *tablespoon lemon juice*
Water	6 *hard-cooked eggs, diced*
Onion	*About ⅛ teaspoon dried dill*
Celery tops	*weed*
Salt	1 *tablespoon chopped fresh*
Pepper	*parsley*

Poach fish in simmering water seasoned with a sliced onion, celery tops, salt, and pepper, just until fish flakes with a fork, about 10 minutes. Carefully lift fish from poaching liquid to warm serving platter; keep warm. Heat butter until it starts to brown. Stir in lemon juice, eggs, dill weed to taste, and parsley. Heat through. Serve sauce hot over poached fish. *Makes 6 servings.*

Mrs. Ekberg enjoyed pondering with us over a definition of the typical Swedish personality. In matters of food, she explained that even the Swedes are counting calories—just a little— enough so they now make this dish with lean pork steaks rather than fresh side pork, as they once did.

BROWNED PORK STEAKS WITH ONION-CREAM GRAVY

2 *medium-sized onions,*	*Salt*
thinly sliced	*Pepper*
About 6 tablespoons butter	2 *tablespoons flour*
4 *very thin lean boneless*	2 *cups milk*
pork steaks	½ *teaspoon prepared mus-*
Flour	*tard*

In a frying pan, slowly sauté onions in about 4 tablespoons of the butter until very tender and brown. Remove onions from frying pan; keep warm. Coat pork steaks in flour seasoned with salt and pepper. Thoroughly brown on both sides in butter remaining in frying pan (add more if necessary). Remove pork to serving platter; keep warm. Scrape drippings loose from bottom of frying pan. Pour off all but 2 tablespoons fat (add butter to make 2 tablespoons, if necessary). Sprinkle in the 2 tablespoons flour; stir to make a smooth paste. Gradually add milk, cooking and stirring to make a smooth sauce. Stir in mustard. Season gravy with salt and pepper. Just before serving, add browned onion. Serve gravy with pork steaks and Spiced Dried Pears (recipe follows). *Makes 4 servings.*

Hot pepper-and-clove-spiced pears make a garnish and condiment for Mrs. Ekberg's browned pork steaks or roast pork.

SPICED DRIED PEARS

12 *moist dried pear halves*
¼ *cup water*
1½ *teaspoons lemon juice*
¼ *cup* each *sugar and butter*

⅛ *teaspoon* each *ground cloves and finely ground black pepper*

Combine in a saucepan pears, water, and lemon juice. Cover and simmer until pears are almost tender. Add sugar, butter, cloves, and pepper. Continue cooking, uncovered, until sugar dissolves and pears are tender; gently turn pears to coat evenly with syrup and spices. Serve warm with pork. *Makes 4 servings.*

One evening we had dinner at Mrs. Ekberg's; this dessert was the superb finale. It is meant to be served out of your loveliest bowl. You might pass sweet cream for those who would soften the full chocolate flavor.

CHOCOLATE MOUSSE

2 egg yolks
Few grains salt
2 cups heavy cream, whipped
1 package (6 ounces) semi-sweet chocolate chips

1 square (1 ounce) unsweetened chocolate
Additional heavy cream (optional)

Beat egg yolks with salt until thick and light-colored; beat into whipped cream. Heat chocolate chips and unsweetened chocolate in top of double boiler, over hot water, just until melted. Stirring briskly with each addition, add chocolate to cream mixture, a large spoonful at a time. Stir until blended and smooth. Turn into serving bowl (about 1½-quart size). Chill in refrigerator at least 1 hour or until ready to serve. If you wish, whip additional cream, pipe through a force bag, and make a decorative pattern on top of mousse. Or pass cream. *Makes 10 servings.*

Out of the yellowed pages of her grandmother's cookbook came Mrs. Ekberg's recipe for this favorite of rural Sweden. You must use a light-colored, dry beer.

SAILORS' BEEF
(*Sjömansbiff*)

2 medium-sized onions, sliced
¼ cup butter
1 pound bottom round steak,
    sliced ¼ inch thick
Flour
Salt
Pepper
3 medium-sized potatoes,
    peeled and thinly sliced
1½ cups (12-ounce can)
    light beer

In a frying pan, sauté onions in about half of the butter until limp; remove from pan and set aside. Coat steak slices in flour seasoned with salt and pepper. Melt remaining butter in frying pan. Add meat slices and quickly brown on both sides. Arrange one third of the potato slices in bottom of a casserole with cover (about 2½-quart size). Sprinkle with salt and pepper to taste; top with a layer of half the sautéed onions, then half the meat. Repeat layering once more and top with remaining one third potato slices, seasoning with salt and pepper. Pour beer over casserole contents. Cover and bake in a very slow oven (250°) for 3 hours or until potatoes and meat are very tender. *Makes 4 servings.*

Leave it to a Hungarian cook to bake the most cloud-like sour cream crêpes in butter—just on one side—then stack them for dessert, layering the creamy side of each with a confection of ground nuts and sugar.

Mrs. Ekberg saw to it that this scheme found its way to her Stockholm kitchen, repeating a preparation she had often observed in her childhood, performed by her family's Hungarian cook.

HUNGARIAN DESSERT CRÊPES

3 eggs, separated
3 tablespoons sugar
½ cup each milk and commercial sour cream
½ cup flour
2 tablespoons cornstarch
2 teaspoons baking powder
¼ teaspoon salt

About 3 tablespoons butter
1 cup coarsely ground (or finely chopped) walnuts
½ cup sugar
½ cup chilled commercial sour cream
Chopped walnuts

In a large mixing bowl, beat egg yolks with the 3 tablespoons sugar until light. Mix in milk and ½ cup sour cream. Sift flour, measure, and sift with cornstarch, baking powder, and salt into mixing bowl. Combine thoroughly. Beat egg whites until stiff but not dry; gently fold into egg-yolk mixture. Heat a small amount of butter in a crêpe pan or shallow frying pan (about 6 inches in diameter). Spoon in enough batter to spread thinly over bottom of pan. Bake on one side only over medium–high heat. Slip crêpe onto a warm platter; sprinkle evenly with part of a mixture of ground walnuts and the ½ cup sugar. Keep warm in oven as you continue baking crêpes, sprinkling with nut-sugar mixture, and stacking one on top of another, until all batter is used. Bake last crêpe on both sides. To serve, cut stack of crêpes into wedges. Pass a bowl of chilled sour cream, sprinkled with chopped nuts, to be spooned over each serving. *Makes 6 servings.*

"Hiram" is a well-liked personality all over Sweden. She writes in a big Stockholm newspaper about food (and poodle dogs, the neighbors, the talk of the day).

Swedish men sing her praises for "Hiram's Tart." It tastes, just as she says, "crisp and charming of butterscotch," for when baked, the pastry rounds will be slightly brown with burned sugar. If it's in any way possible, when you serve Hiram's tart, also serve icy-cold fresh strawberries, sprinkled with a little rum.

HIRAM'S TART

¼ *package yeast (active dry*
or compressed)
2 *tablespoons lukewarm*
water
⅔ *cup butter*

1⅓ *cups flour*
1 *cup heavy cream*
⅓ *cup sugar*
Rum or vanilla

Sprinkle or crumble yeast into water; stir to dissolve. With pastry blender or two knives, cut butter into flour in a large mixing bowl until particles are fine. Add yeast mixture and 2 tablespoons of the cream; toss with a fork to mix. Gather mixture together into a ball. Wrap in waxed paper or foil and chill about 30 minutes or until dough can be rolled out. On a lightly floured board, roll out dough very thin. Cut into four 8-inch rounds. Gently lift each round onto baking sheet; prick with a fork. Sprinkle each round with sugar. Bake in a hot oven (400°) for 10 minutes or until golden. Gently slip onto wire racks to cool. At serving time, whip remaining cream with rum or vanilla to taste. Spread one third of the cream on one cooled pastry round, one third on another round (save remaining cream for topping); top each with a plain pastry round. With a sharp, thin-bladed knife, cut into wedges to serve. Use remaining cream to decoratively pipe through force bag or spoon on top of each serving. *Makes 8 to 10 servings.*

When Hiram entertains at home, the food is important, but
the guests more so. So the food is devastating to eat—but
quick to contrive.

First course is often hot wine bouillon served in Swedish
ceramic pots. A bowl of fluffy Italian *Pesto*, with its potent
cheese-garlic seasoning, is passed. Each guest drops a spoonful on top of his steaming soup. The sauce melts, sending up
a waft of warm pungency.

WINE BOUILLON AL PESTO

> 3 *tablespoons butter*
> 4 *tablespoons freshly grated*
>   *Parmesan cheese*
> 1 *teaspoon crumbled dried*
>   *sweet basil*
> 1 *clove garlic, minced or*
>   *mashed*

> 1 *can (about 10½-ounce*
>   *size) beef bouillon*
> *Water*
> 2 *tablespoons dry red or*
>   *white table wine or sherry*

Beat butter until creamy; beat in cheese, basil, and garlic.
Pile mixture into small serving dish. Heat canned bouillon with
water as directed on can until very hot. Just before serving, stir
in wine. Serve in hot soup bowls. Pass sauce. *Makes 4 servings.*

For the *pièce de résistance*, a fine broiled steak sits upon a
bed of sautéed celery. The sauce is original—angostura bitters,
whipped sweet cream, crisp brown pan drippings.

BROILED STEAK WITH ANGOSTURA CREAM TOPPING

> 8 *stalks celery, cut in diago-*
>   *nal slices ⅛-inch thick*
> 2 *medium-sized onions,*
>   *thinly sliced*
> ¼ *cup butter*

> *Salt*
> *Pepper*
> 4 *broiling steaks*
> ½ *teaspoon angostura bitters*
> ½ *cup heavy cream, whipped*

Slowly sauté celery and onions in butter until tender-crisp, about 15 minutes. Season with salt and pepper. Meanwhile, broil steaks to the doneness you desire; season with salt and pepper. At serving time, arrange sautéed celery in a bed on each of four heated plates; place broiled steaks on top of celery. Fold angostura bitters into whipped cream along with brown drippings from steak broiling pan. Top each steak with a spoonful of the seasoned whipped cream. Serve immediately. *Makes 4 servings.*

If it's not Hiram's Tart for dessert, it's likely to be liqueured fresh fruit enfolded in an apricot meringue. A fresh blossom tops each serving.

MERINGUE-MARBLED FRUIT BOWL

2 cups fresh apricot slices
2 cups fresh red raspberries   ½ cup apricot jam
1 cup blueberries   ¼ cup light corn syrup
½ cup cointreau or curaçao   8 washed fresh flower blos-
2 egg whites   soms

Combine apricots, raspberries, and blueberries in a bowl; sprinkle with cointreau or curaçao. Chill thoroughly, at least 1 hour; occasionally turn fruits gently in liqueur. Beat egg whites until stiff but not dry. Mix jam and syrup; gradually beat into egg whites. Beat until stiff peaks form. Drain off and save all liquid from chilled fruits. Gently and partially fold egg-white mixture into fruits. Turn into large serving bowl or individual dessert glasses. Decorate with flower blossoms. Chill 30 minutes. At serving time, pass liqueur drained from fruits to be sprinkled over each serving. *Makes 8 servings.*

Swedish home baking reaches its peak in the creation of the eggy sweet yeast dough. Usually, it's fashioned into fancy coffee braids. But the best way we ever tasted it was in the form of poppy-seed-topped crescents—split, and enclosing thin, thin slices of Swiss cheese. The time was morning; the scene— a sunny breakfast table set with dainty napkins, flowers, and a big pot of Swedish coffee.

Try these with morning coffee or afternoon tea, when your freshly baked rolls are still a little warm. You'll taste the sweetness of the yeasty bread, the saltiness of the butter in it, the sharpness of aged Swiss cheese.

POPPY SEED
BUTTER CRESCENTS

2 packages yeast (*active dry or compressed*)
½ cup water (*warm for dry yeast, lukewarm for compressed*)
2 cups milk, scalded
1 cup (2 sticks) butter
1 cup sugar
¾ teaspoon salt
1 teaspoon grated lemon peel
2 egg yolks, beaten

About 8 cups flour
4 tablespoons melted butter
1 egg white, beaten
About 2 teaspoons poppy seeds
Natural Swiss cheese, thinly sliced

Sprinkle or crumble yeast into water; stir until dissolved. Pour hot milk into large mixing bowl. Add butter in pieces, and stir until melted. Stir in sugar, salt, and lemon peel. When cooled to lukewarm, stir in egg yolks. Stir in 2 cups of the flour; beat until smooth. Add yeast mixture and enough additional flour to make a moderately firm dough; beat with a spoon until smooth. Cover and let rise in a warm place until doubled in bulk, about 2 hours. Punch down. Divide dough into 4 parts. On a lightly floured board, roll each part into a 10-inch circle. Brush with melted butter. Cut into 8 wedges. Roll up each piece, starting at wide end. Place on a greased baking sheet, folded edge down. Allow to rise in a warm place until almost doubled in bulk, about 1 hour. Gently brush with beaten egg white; sprinkle with poppy seeds. Bake in a hot oven (425°) for 10 minutes or until golden brown. Remove to wire rack to cool slightly. Split and fill with overlapping cheese slices. *Makes 36 crescent sandwiches.*

The opportunity came to try a sauna, and we reasoned that a little steam treatment might well offset the effects of our caloric intake. Whisked into a little cubicle, we threw off our drip-drys and timidly approached the steam room. There we found wooden risers (it gets hotter as you ascend!) and fleshy ladies chattering gayly and beating themselves with birch branches. Soon we grasped the routine: you roast yourself to the fainting point, whiz through a soapy shower, and plunge into a pool of ice water. A luxurious "extra"—a tingly massage with a lathered bristly brush, and a dousing with buckets of warm water.

THE ICEY PLUNGE

THE SAUNA CYCLE

Still limp from our sauna, we looked to a salubrious meal to revive our strength. While dining, we encountered a spirited international pair, the Trubys. Anne's American husband, Hank, thrives on her Swedish cooking—especially her chicken-and-mushroom-filled crêpes. They might be served for luncheon or dinner—but better yet, late at night, with beer or wine.

Part of the reason for the extra-good chicken filling is that the chicken is first sautéed to a golden brown, then cut into bites to go with mushrooms. In baking, the crêpes should get slightly crisp under their cheese topping—a little like enchiladas, according to Hank.

CHICKEN-AND-MUSHROOM CRÊPES

2 eggs
1 cup milk
⅔ cup flour
¼ teaspoon salt
About ¼ cup butter
½ broiler-fryer (about 2½ pounds), cut into pieces (or 1¼ cups small pieces of boned chicken meat)
Salt
Pepper

3 tablespoons (or more) butter
½ pound fresh mushrooms, sliced
3 tablespoons sliced green onions
3 tablespoons heavy cream
½ pound mild natural cheese (mild Cheddar, Tybo, Jack, Gouda, Edam, Gruyère), shredded

Make crêpes: Beat eggs and stir in milk. Sift flour, measure, and sift again with salt into egg mixture; beat until smooth. Melt a small amount of butter in an 8-inch frying pan. Pour in about ¼ cup of the thin batter; turn and tilt pan so batter covers entire surface. Cook until light brown on both sides; slip crêpe out of pan onto clean towel. Continue until all batter is used, making 8 crêpes.

Sprinkle chicken with salt and pepper to taste. Sauté in butter until brown; continue to cook until done. Remove chicken meat from bone; cut into small pieces. In same frying pan, sauté mushrooms and onions until tender (add more butter if necessary). Mix chicken meat, mushrooms, onion, and cream. Season with salt and pepper. Put a spoonful of the chicken mixture in center of each crêpe, roll up, and place in a greased baking pan (about 7 by 11 inches). Sprinkle shredded cheese over top. Bake in a moderate oven (350°) for 30 minutes. *Makes 4 servings.*

A preamble to another of Anne's dishes was the entrancing aroma while it baked.

NUT-STUFFED BURGUNDY HAM ROLLS

12 thin slices baked or boiled ham (about 1½ pounds meat)
1 cup dry red table wine
¼ cup butter

⅓ cup sliced green onions with tops
1⅓ cups finely chopped walnuts
2 cups shredded sharp Cheddar cheese
1 cup heavy cream

Marinate ham slices in wine in refrigerator 12 hours or overnight. Heat butter in a frying pan. In it sauté all but 2 tablespoons of the green onions with the nuts until onions are limp and nuts slightly toasted. Remove from heat, add 1½ cups of the cheese, and toss to mix. Remove ham from wine. Place a spoonful of the cheese stuffing on each ham slice, roll up, fasten with tooth-picks, if necessary, and place rolls in a single layer on a greased shallow baking dish. Pour cream evenly over rolls. Bake in a slow oven (300°) for 30 minutes, basting rolls occasionally with the cream. After 30 minutes, sprinkle ham rolls with remaining cheese and return to oven for 10 minutes or until cheese is melted. Just before serving, sprinkle with remaining green onions. *Makes 6 servings.*

Fru Ohlsson is an impeccable cook. She carefully singled out one recipe and presented it to us in written form. We would deprive you of the Swedish cook's personality if we didn't let you cook from this recipe, directly translated.

SWEDISH CUTLETS (OR CHOPS)

Though lamb chops are preferred, veal cutlets or pork chops are almost as nice. Rub a little garlic salt into the meat, if you like that flavor. Add salt and pepper to taste and sauté the chops in a skillet until well browned. Remove to a sizzling platter, pouring on the juice from the pan. (Now comes the thrilling touch!) Place on each chop a heaping teaspoonful of finely minced onion, and over that a generous slice of Roquefort cheese. Do not experiment with any other type of cheese. When the chops have remained in a hot oven for about 10 minutes, the cheese and onion will have produced a very tasty sauce.

Barbro, an attractive Swedish girl and budding fashion journalist, tempted us with her description of *Krabbgott*, which means "something good of crab." She serves it as a dish "nice and hot to eat as you talk"—late in the evening. Best accompaniments are glasses of dry red wine, bread, butter, and cheese. Adjust the amount of curry to suit your tastes, but Barbro recommends enough "so you really feel it."

SWEDISH CRAB WITH CURRY
(*Krabbgott*)

3 tablespoons butter	1 can (about 1 pound) solid-pack tomatoes
¾ cup regular rice	½ teaspoon lemon juice
1½ cups bouillon	Dash each salt and pepper
2 teaspoons finely chopped onions	1½ cups (about ¾ pound) flaked crab meat
½ teaspoon (or more) curry powder	

Melt half the butter in a saucepan, add rice, and heat and stir until toasted and golden. Add bouillon, cover, and cook over low heat 20 minutes or until rice is tender. Meantime, sauté onions in remaining butter until limp. Stir in curry powder. Add tomatoes, lemon juice, salt, and pepper. Cook and stir over medium heat about 15 minutes. Just before serving, add crab meat; heat through. At serving time, bring rice to table in large serving container. Turn tomato-crab sauce over rice. Let stand a few moments for juices to mingle with rice. Gently stir to mix. Spoon onto warm serving plates. *Makes 4 generous servings.*

The night we were Barbro's guests, we had "something good of" cheese and cream and eggs and radishes baked together in a buttery tart shell. No amount of warning can prepare you for its utter richness! Serve this late at night with dry red wine and candlelight.

BARBRO'S CHEESE-AND-CREAM TART

1 cup flour	4 egg yolks
½ cup (1 stick) butter	¾ cup heavy cream
¾ cup shredded Cheddar, Edam, Gouda, or Gruyère cheese	¼ teaspoon salt
¼ cup heavy cream	¼ cup thinly sliced red radishes

Sift and measure flour into mixing bowl. With a pastry blender, cut butter into flour until particles are coarse. Stir in ½ cup of the cheese. Pour in the ¼ cup cream; toss mixture with a fork until all parts are moistened. Turn into a 9-inch round pie pan or shallow baking pan. With floured fingertips, press mixture into bottom and sides of pan. Prick with tines of a floured fork. Bake in a hot oven (425°) for 10 to 12 minutes. (The sides will slip down a little during baking.) Cool on wire rack. Sprinkle remaining cheese evenly over bottom of cooled tart shell. Beat together egg yolks, the ¾ cup cream, and salt. Pour egg mixture over cheese. Sprinkle radish slices evenly over top. Bake in a slow oven (325°) for 20 to 25 minutes or until custard is set. Cut tart into wedges and serve hot. *Makes 6 servings.*

Variation: You might decorate the top with red pimiento strips instead of radishes.

Note to the reader: We hope you won't be hopelessly muddled by our geographical jumps. Following our first visit to Stockholm, we went directly to Norway, and at the end of our trip, came back to Stockholm by way of Mora and Uppsala.

Driving south along the edge of Lake Siljan on our first evening back in Sweden, we found ourselves in Mora, home of the renowned painter, Anders Zorn. Curiosity brought us to the doorstep of a house marked "RUM" (room?). On a brief tour of our night's new quarters, the rather hefty landlady, demonstrating concern for our well-being, gracefully planted one foot in the middle of the bathtub and slammed the window shut.

In Uppsala, an impressive tour of the university and cathedral preceded an interview with a young homemaker. Kept in perpetual motion as she trailed the escapades of two young sons, she recalled Swedish foods of her childhood. Summer days at her grandmother's place in the country often meant a savory hot sandwich for supper.

SWEDISH SANDWICH FROM A SUMMER PLACE

8 *strips lean bacon, cut into crosswise strips about ¼-inch wide*

2 *cups coarsely shredded potatoes*

2 *large tomatoes, seeded and diced*

¼ *cup diced dill pickle*

4 *slices firm-textured white bread*

About ½ *cup (1 stick) butter, melted*

4 *eggs*

Salt

Freshly ground black pepper

Crisp salad greens

Cook bacon in frying pan until crisp; drain on absorbent paper towels. Add potatoes to hot bacon fat remaining in frying pan; sauté until golden brown and crisp. Add tomatoes, dill pickle, and bacon bits, and continue to cook, carefully stirring to mix, just until mixture is heated through. Meanwhile brush bread on both sides with melted butter. Quickly grill or toast on both sides. Place toast slices on each of 4 individual warmed plates. Top each with one fourth of the potato mixture; keep warm. Fry eggs on one side in butter. Place an egg on top of each sandwich. Sprinkle with salt and black pepper. Garnish plates with salad greens. Serve immediately. *Makes 4 sandwiches.*

Exhilarated by the thought of another taste of Stockholm, we quickly found accommodations at the home of a retired couple, the Hedemans. We dropped our baggage and fled to the center of the city for a snack at Kungsträdgården Park.

Licking off the last bite of hot dog, we slipped into our white gloves and sprinted around the corner to the Royal Opera House and a night of Verdi. Shirley, a fair-weather Californian, thought she felt a draft when a door opened on the stage set thousands of feet below.

During the intermission we made friends with a stocky intellectual from Cairo. It isn't easy to give an illusion of *savoir-faire* while puffing on a long, fat Egyptian "Presidente" cigarette.

Next morning we exchanged recipes with our charitable hostess. Fru Hedeman told us that when her daughter first got married, she was "not so clever to cook," so her mother taught her to make this dish for special occasions—a sure success.

BEEF-AND-MUSHROOM PARMESAN

½ pound fresh mushrooms,
　sliced
6 tablespoons butter
1½ pounds sliced eye of beef
　round, pounded very thin
　(or tenderloin or sirloin
　sliced very thin)
Salt

Pepper
½ cup shredded or grated
　Parmesan cheese
2 teaspoons flour
⅔ cup beef bouillon
½ cup dry white table wine
Tomato wedges

Sauté mushrooms in 2 tablespoons of the butter until tender; set aside; keep warm. Sprinkle meat slices on one side with salt and pepper to taste. In a large frying pan, brown meat slices quickly on both sides in remaining butter. Sprinkle each slice with cheese and arrange slices, overlapping, on serving platter. Keep warm in moderate (350°) oven. Scrape loose the drippings remaining in frying pan. Stir in flour to make a smooth paste. Gradually add bouillon, then wine, cooking and stirring to make a smooth, thin sauce. Pour sauce over meat slices. Turn sautéed mushrooms over top of meat. Return meat to oven and heat for 10 minutes. Garnish serving platter with tomato wedges. *Makes 6 servings.*

Friends in San Francisco told us to look up the Cronins in Stockholm. When we met Mrs. Cronin, she sat right down and told us of all the food occasions her family celebrates. Throughout the household there is a favored food combination held in reserve for two events—Thursday night family dinner and "men's nights" (occasional parties for Mr. Cronin and his men friends only).

The menu is yellow Pea Soup with Pork followed by tiny Swedish Pancakes with Lingonberries or Strawberry Preserves.

PEA SOUP WITH PORK

1½ cups yellow dried split peas
2 quarts water
1 pound pork shoulder meat
2 onions, peeled and thinly sliced
2 carrots, peeled and thinly sliced crosswise
1 leek, thinly sliced crosswise
About 2 teaspoons salt
About ½ teaspoon pepper
1 teaspoon crumbled dried marjoram
Dark prepared mustard

Combine all ingredients except mustard in a large kettle. Cover, heat to boiling; reduce heat and simmer 1½ hours or until pork and peas are tender. Taste and correct seasoning. Remove pork from soup; slice; serve on a separate warm platter. Offer mustard. Ladle hot soup into bowls. *Makes 4 to 6 servings.*

These are the tenderest of pancakes. If you're not confident of your adeptness in handling these delicate, eggy sheets, make them first with just 2 cups milk. As you increase your proficiency and add more milk, the pancakes will get more and more tender. Use a flexible spatula, a pancake turner, or your fingers to help in turning them.

SWEDISH PANCAKES WITH LINGONBERRIES

1 cup flour
2 teaspoons sugar
¼ teaspoon salt
3 eggs
2 to 3 cups milk
About ⅓ cup butter
Lingonberries or strawberry preserves

Sift flour, measure, and sift again with sugar and salt into mixing bowl. In another bowl, beat together eggs and milk. Gradually stir egg-milk mixture into dry ingredients; beat until smooth. Allow to stand 2 hours. Heat Swedish pancake pan (or crêpe pan or shallow frying pan—no larger than 8 inches in diameter); butter well. Beat batter again. Pour 1 tablespoon batter into each pan section (or just enough batter in crêpe pan or frying pan to cover bottom of pan when tilted). Bake over medium heat until golden brown on the bottom, dry-looking on top; turn and brown on second side. (Stir batter occasionally as you bake pancakes.) Place pancakes on very hot platter; serve immediately with lingonberries or strawberry preserves. *Makes 4 servings.*

In Stockholm, one good cook seemed to lead to another. Mrs. Cronin told us we must talk to Mrs. Ternberger (and Mrs. Ternberger later guided us to Mrs. Selander). Accustomed as she is to pleasing foreign guests with her cooking, Mrs. Ternberger furrowed her brow when we asked for a recipe for our cookbook; she feared her recipes might not suit American tastes. Then suddenly she brightened, remembering her Swedish ham-and-egg pancake that "Americans always like."

SWEDISH HAM PANCAKE AMERICANS LIKE

¼ *pound smoked ham, cut into small cubes*	½ *teaspoon dry mustard*
	3 *eggs*
1 *tablespoon butter*	2 *cups milk*
1 *cup flour*	*Currant-Butter Syrup (recipe*
1 *tablespoon sugar*	*below)*
¾ *teaspoon salt*	

Sauté ham in butter in a large frying pan (about 9-inch diameter) until browned. Sift flour, sugar, salt, and dry mustard into a large mixing bowl. Beat eggs slightly, add milk, and beat again to mix; pour into dry ingredients. Mix until blended and smooth. Pour egg mixture over browned ham and butter in frying pan. Place in a moderately hot oven (375°) and bake 30 minutes or until pancake is set and golden. Cut into wedges. Serve immediately with Currant-Butter Syrup. *Makes 6 servings.*

Currant-Butter Syrup: Over low heat, melt together 1½ tablespoons butter and ⅓ cup red currant jelly. Ladle over pancake wedges.

It was Mrs. Ternberger who first described the Selander family's Christmas activities. Every year Mother and Father Selander and a houseful of young Selanders hold a Christmas cooky-making in their Stockholm kitchen. The event means spicy ginger cookies—cut out in all sorts of whimsical storybook shapes. The recipe is part of their family history.

SWEDISH CHRISTMAS GINGER SNAPS
(*Pepparkakor*)

> ¾ cup (1½ sticks) butter,
>   cut into small pieces
> ¼ cup water
> 1¼ cups brown sugar, firmly
>   packed
> 1½ teaspoons each ground
>   cinnamon, ginger, and
>   cloves
> 2 cups flour
> ¼ teaspoon baking soda
> 2 egg whites
> 1 teaspoon vanilla
> About 4 cups sifted pow-
>   dered sugar

Put butter into a large mixing bowl. Combine water, brown sugar, cinnamon, ginger, and cloves in a saucepan. Heat to boiling;

boil 1 minute, stirring. Pour hot spice mixture over butter; stir to melt butter. Sift flour, measure 2 cups, and sift again with baking soda. Add to spice mixture; stir to blend thoroughly. Cover dough tightly or wrap in waxed paper or aluminum foil. Chill in refrigerator 12 hours or overnight. Cut off small, workable portions of dough. Roll each out very thin (about ⅛-inch thick) on a lightly floured board. Cut into shapes with fancy cooky cutters. With flexible spatula, lift cookies onto greased baking sheet. Bake in a moderately hot oven (375°) about 8 minutes or until lightly browned. Cool on wire racks. Make icing: Beat egg whites until stiff but not dry. Beat in vanilla and enough powdered sugar so that mixture holds soft peaks when beater is lifted. Spoon icing into force bag. Decorate cooled cookies. *Makes about 5 dozen cookies.*

Variation: Do not roll out chilled dough. Instead, pinch off small portions and roll, between palms, into balls about ¾-inch in diameter. Drop balls into granulated sugar to coat all sides. Bake as for cut-out cookies.

FISH AND FJORDS IN NORWAY

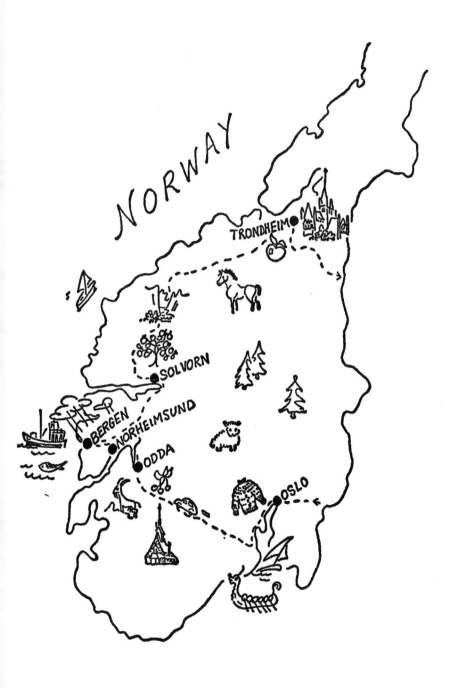

The Norwegian border officials greeted us, and we made a beeline for Oslo—as much of a beeline as can be made while readjusting to driving on the right-hand side of roads that twist through beautiful, unfamiliar terrain.

In Oslo, with an eye to our dwindling kroner supply, we put ourselves under the fiercely protective care of the Salvation Army Resident Home for Girls. Breakfast included three kinds of cheese, meat, radishes, cucumbers, heart-shaped waffles—plus inviting-looking crusty slices of . . . French toast? We loaded our plates with huge portions. With the first bite, spirits sank—it was mush!

Shirley, riffling through the pages of all the Norwegian cookbooks in a bookstore, attracted a lady of similar food passions. She turned out to be a bookstore clerk, the busy mother of a growing family, and a good cook. She revealed her way with wintertime lamb stew, fresh salmon, and spring asparagus.

LAMB CHOP-AND-MUSHROOM STEW

4 shoulder lamb chops, well-trimmed	About ¼ cup butter
Salt	½ pound fresh mushroom caps
Pepper	1 clove garlic, minced or mashed
Flour	
1 medium-sized onion, peeled and chopped	½ cup dry red table wine
	Hot steamed rice or noodles

Season lamb chops with salt and pepper to taste; coat both sides with flour. In a large frying pan, quickly brown the chops on both sides in a small amount of the butter. Remove chops and set aside. In the same pan, sauté onion in remaining drippings until golden (add butter if necessary). Arrange browned meat on top of onions. Meanwhile, melt remaining butter, add mushrooms, lift and turn mushrooms to brown slightly, and coat all sides with butter. Turn mushrooms and butter over chops. Combine garlic and all but 1 tablespoon of the wine; pour over meat. Cover pan and simmer 30 minutes or until lamb is very tender. Just before serving, sprinkle remaining wine into stew. Serve each chop over a bed of steamed rice or buttered noodles, garnish with mushroom caps, ladle pan juices over top. *Makes 4 servings.*

Norwegian cooks take much pleasure in presenting a whole fish on a handsome serving platter designed especially for that purpose. However, a smaller portion of fish will do. Serve this masked fish for an appetizer course, or on a luncheon buffet table.

CHILLED SALMON WITH SOUR CREAM-HORSERADISH SAUCE

About 1 quart water
1 onion, sliced
Celery tops
About 4 peppercorns
Salt
2- to 2½-pound salmon fillet
1 cup commercial sour cream

1 teaspoon lemon juice
½ to ¾ teaspoon prepared
horseradish
¼ teaspoon salt
⅛ teaspoon pepper
Lemon slices
Fresh parsley sprigs

In a large saucepan, simmer water, onion, celery tops, peppercorns, and salt until broth is well seasoned, about 30 minutes. Strain through a fine sieve; return broth to saucepan. Simmer salmon in broth just until it flakes with a fork, about 12 minutes. Remove salmon to a platter and chill thoroughly. Before serving, mix together sour cream, lemon juice, horseradish, the ¼ teaspoon salt, and pepper. Spread evenly over chilled salmon. Garnish platter with lemon slices and parsley sprigs. *Makes 6 main-dish servings or 10 appetizers.*

Note: To poach a whole salmon, about 6 or 7 pounds, triple recipe and follow procedure above except: Wrap fish in cheesecloth and place in a large shallow pan. Cover with broth. Bake in a moderate oven (350°) until thick part of fish flakes when broken with a fork, about 25 to 30 minutes. While fish is still warm, remove cheesecloth; carefully pull off skin; remove fins; chill.

This spring-vegetable dish is best of all if you grate whole nutmegs into the butter for tender spears of asparagus, as the Norwegians do. (But prepared ground nutmeg will taste good, too.)

ASPARAGUS WITH NUTMEG-BROWNED BUTTER

2 *pounds fresh asparagus*   *Salt*
    spears (or 2 packages, 10   6 *tablespoons butter*
    ounces each, *frozen as-*   ¼ *teaspoon grated or ground*
    paragus spears)   *nutmeg*
Boiling salted water

Wash and trim fresh asparagus spears. Cook fresh or frozen spears in a small amount of boiling salted water just until tender. Drain thoroughly. Season lightly with salt; turn into serving dish. In a small pan, heat butter until it bubbles and browns slightly; stir in nutmeg. Pour butter over asparagus. Serve immediately. *Makes 6 servings.*

In the mood for a bit of night life, we donned our high heels and headed for Oslo's Metropol Jazz Center. Dance partners for the evening included a short, moustached man from Saudi Arabia, a waist-high civil engineer from Hong Kong, a sleepy-looking German, and a gangly Norwegian (who won our instant affections by treating us to Peach Melba).

Digressing momentarily from things gastronomic, we stopped at the National Art Gallery. We were enthralled by the depth of feeling expressed in the character studies of Christian Krohg, a Norwegian turn-of-the-century painter (but found we were no longer able to pass by those fleshy Rubens ladies without a twinge of self-consciousness!).

We wandered into a department store, met a gracious young clerk, and accepted her invitation to dinner.

Next evening, surrounded by her jovial family, we were served a dish of lamb and cabbage. We ate eagerly—pepper-

corns and all. Disgrace! The younger sister, noting our to-
tally empty plates, let out a startled squeal. Between giggles,
she sputtered, "Only stout men with great arm muscles eat
the peppercorns!"

This is an autumn dish all over Norway, when the cabbage
is ready to harvest and the sheep are ready for market. Here
is how you make it—but don't eat the peppercorns!

LAMB-AND-CABBAGE PEPPER POT
(*Fårikål*)

5 *strips bacon, cut into small pieces*	4 *teaspoons whole peppercorns*
1 *medium-sized onion, peeled and sliced*	1 *large head white cabbage*
1½ *pounds boneless lamb stew meat*	4 *tomatoes, peeled and cut into wedges*
Salt	2 *teaspoons salt*
Flour	*Hot boiled potatoes topped with melted butter and freshly chopped parsley*
¾ *cup water*	

In a frying pan, sauté bacon and onion slices until bacon is
almost crisp and onions are limp. Remove bacon and onions to
a kettle with cover. Sprinkle lamb pieces with salt to taste. Dust
on all sides with flour. Quickly brown lamb on all sides in
bacon drippings remaining in frying pan. Add browned meat to
kettle along with water and peppercorns. Cover and simmer 1
hour or until lamb is tender. Remove meat from kettle. Cut
cabbage into 4 wedges; remove core; cut each wedge in half,
crosswise; break leaves apart. Arrange cabbage leaves, meat, and
tomatoes in layers (sprinkle cabbage and tomatoes with salt), beginning and ending with cabbage. Cover pan. Cook 30 minutes
more or until cabbage is tender. Turn into a heated tureen; ladle
onto hot plates. Serve with boiled potatoes. *Makes 6 servings.*

We departed from Oslo, aimed our car in a westwardly direction, and braced ourselves for narrow roads and our first glimpse of a fjord.

At one point we rounded a bend, and there on a bleak mountaintop we found a large herd of goateed creatures

lounging on the rocks. We scrambled out to make their acquaintance and came back to find gregarious Alfred in the car—hopping from front to back seat, licking the steering wheel, nibbling on luggage, finally settling in the front seat ready to chauffeur us down the mountain.

Alfred's languid companions can take some credit for the following pheasant recipe; a little bit of *Gjetost*—that Norwegian goat's-milk cheese that looks like a chunk of caramel—is the unexpected ingredient that gives the slightly burnt sugar taste to the sauce. Don't be apprehensive when you see the cream curdling around the bird as it simmers—it's supposed to.

A tart Norwegian red berry (*Tyttebær*) sauce should be the accompanying fruit relish; lacking this, whole cranberries in sauce are an excellent substitute. And, if you haven't snared a pheasant, you can substitute a chicken.

PHEASANT IN
GJETOST CREAM SAUCE

1 pheasant (or 1 frying chicken, about 3 pounds), cut into pieces	1 cup heavy cream
	1 tablespoon flour
	About 1 cup milk
Salt	¼ cup shredded Gjetost cheese
Pepper	
¼ cup (½ stick) butter	Vinegar (optional)

Sprinkle pheasant pieces with salt and pepper to taste. In a heavy frying pan with cover, quickly brown pheasant pieces on all sides in melted butter. Reduce heat to low. Pour cream over pheasant pieces. Cover and cook over low heat about 1 hour or until pheasant is very tender; turn pieces and stir cream in bottom of pan occasionally. Remove pheasant to hot serving platter. Mix flour to a paste with a little of the milk. Stir into simmering liquid remaining in frying pan; cook and stir over low heat to blend. Gradually add milk, stirring to make a smooth sauce. Just before serving, stir in cheese; continue heating just until cheese is melted and blended. Taste sauce and correct seasoning. Stir in a few drops vinegar, if you wish. Turn sauce into gravy boat. Pass it to ladle over pheasant pieces. *Makes 4 servings.*

Note: Vinegar gives a slightly sweet-sour character to the sauce; add it if you prefer a sharper poultry sauce.

The route to Bergen involved a path through Odda and an overnight stop at the Odda Pension. Undaunted by an article we had just read, "From Gorger to Gorgeous," we hastened to the pension dining room and seated ourselves at a long

table with four non-English-speaking gentlemen. Apparently our silent supper companions had eaten the usual Norwegian *"middag"* shortly before, for after a few meager sandwiches, their activity subsided. They watched with disbelief as the two of us, in a more ravenous mood, kept pointing to new delicacies to be passed our way.

Barbara, in an effort to redeem herself, thought she would at least show that she had mastered the Scandinavian cheese knife. But, alas! Each piece came off in a limp and shriveled shred!

At that same tense table, we did gather our nervous wits enough to realize that we were tasting an extraordinary preserve—spicy with berries and rhubarb, tangy with orange.

ORANGE-RHUBARB-RASPBERRY JAM

2 oranges	1 pound rhubarb, cut into
½ lemon	½-inch pieces
Water	1 cup raspberries
1½ cups sugar	1 cup sugar
⅓ cup water	

Cover oranges and lemon with water. Cover and simmer 3 hours. Let fruits stand in water overnight. Next day, cut fruits in quarters. Spoon out pulp and save; discard seeds. Cut peel into fine, even slivers. Combine pulp, peel, the 1½ cups sugar, and the ⅓ cup water. Simmer 45 minutes, or until liquid is honeylike in consistency, stirring constantly. Meanwhile, in another saucepan, combine rhubarb, raspberries, and the 1 cup sugar. Slowly bring to a boil, stirring. Continue to cook, stirring, until thick. Combine rhubarb mixture thoroughly with orange mixture. Heat to a full rolling boil. Ladle into hot sterilized glasses and seal. *Makes about four 8-ounce glasses.*

After our feast, we set out on a bracing twilight walk and wound up in a discussion with a flirtatious hotel proprietor. We slyly averted his amorous thoughts with an academic inquisition, and learned of blueberry erêpes, fried trout, fruit soups.

Blueberries grow wild on the rugged fjord mountain-sides in Norway. Sweetened with sugar, they then fill folded breakfast crêpes to plumpness. As you eat, you sprinkle crêpes with powdered sugar and squeeze on fresh lemon juice. (They're fine for dessert, too.)

BLUEBERRY BREAKFAST CRÊPES

3 eggs
1 cup milk
1½ tablespoons melted butter
¾ cup flour
1 tablespoon sugar
¼ teaspoon salt

About 3 tablespoons butter
1½ cups fresh blueberries
Granulated sugar
Sifted powdered sugar
Lemon wedges
Warm melted butter (optional)

Beat eggs well. Beat in milk and butter. Sift flour, measure, and sift again with sugar and salt into egg mixture; beat until smooth. Heat a shallow frying pan (about 8 inches in diameter); butter well. Pour in about 3 tablespoons batter; turn and tilt pan so batter covers entire surface. Bake until golden brown on both sides. Spoon about 3 tablespoons of the blueberries, sweetened to taste with granulated sugar, in center of crêpe; fold in half and lift to a heated plate; keep warm. Repeat, buttering pan before baking each crêpe. Serve about two filled crêpes to each person. Pass powdered sugar and lemon wedges and melted butter, if you wish. *Makes 4 servings.*

When mid-August comes, waters from the high mountains bring down fresh trout—and the people of the meadow towns below get set for trout fried in sour cream.

SOUR CREAM FRIED TROUT

4 fresh trout (or 4 frozen trout)	¼ cup (½ stick) butter
Salt	¾ cup commercial sour cream
Flour	Parsley sprigs, lemon wedges for garnish
Pepper	

Clean fresh trout; do not fillet (allow frozen trout to thaw). Sprinkle fish cavities with salt. Dust outside of fish with flour seasoned with salt and pepper. Melt butter in frying pan; add trout; quickly fry on both sides over medium heat until golden brown (about 5 minutes each side). Spoon sour cream over fish; turn fish to coat all sides. Remove to warm serving plate. Continue to heat sour cream and butter remaining in frying pan until cream curdles; stir to blend; pour over fish. Garnish platter with parsley sprigs and lemon wedges. Serve immediately. *Makes 4 servings.*

In the cold of winter, Norwegians sometimes serve their sweet dessert soups warm rather than chilled. For this, the best fruits are cherries or purple plums.

The topping on the cherry soup is a whip of *Kummin-ost* cheese, heavily peppered with caraway seeds. Float whipped cream, dusted with nutmeg, on top of a steaming plum-rum soup.

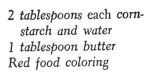

CHERRY SOUP WITH
KUMMIN-OST TOPPING

> *2 cans (1 pound each) pitted*
> *tart red cherries*
> *¾ cup sugar*
> *3 lemon slices*
> *⅛ teaspoon each cinnamon*
> *and cloves*

2 tablespoons each corn-
starch and water
1 tablespoon butter
Red food coloring

Drain and save liquid from cherries. Measure 1 cup of the liquid into a saucepan. Add sugar, lemon slices, cinnamon, and cloves, and bring to a boil. Add cherries and bring to a boil again. Blend cornstarch and water and stir into cherries. Stir gently and bring to a boil once more. Stir in butter and a few drops of red food coloring. Remove lemon slices. Ladle soup into serving bowls, and top each with a dollop of the cheese whip (recipe below). *Makes 6 servings.*

Kummin-ost Whip: Shred 8 ounces *Kummin-ost* cheese into mixing bowl. Beat, gradually adding ½ cup heavy cream, until mixture is smooth and fluffy.

HOT PLUM-RUM SOUP

1 large can (1 pound, 14 ounces) purple plums in heavy syrup
¼ cup brown sugar, firmly packed
1 tablespoon cornstarch
½ teaspoon lemon juice

Few grains salt
1 tablespoon butter
1 tablespoon rum
Few drops red food coloring (optional)
⅓ cup heavy cream, whipped
Nutmeg

Drain and measure syrup from plums; save 1 cup. Remove pits from plums. Whirl plums in a blender until smooth (or press through food mill to make a purée). Mix together in a saucepan the brown sugar and cornstarch. Add the 1 cup plum syrup, lemon juice, and salt. Cook over medium heat, stirring, until mixture is smooth and slightly thickened. Stir in puréed plums; heat through. Add butter and rum; stir to melt butter. Add food coloring, if you wish. Ladle soup into small soup bowls or sherbet glasses. Top each serving with a spoonful of whipped cream sprinkled with nutmeg. *Makes 6 servings.*

The frail but spunky old lady who insisted on toting our suitcases up to our third-floor hotel room in Norheimsund had additional help to offer when we mentioned our cookbook.

In Norway, this sour cream porridge carries much significance. It is most exalted as a festival food, traditional for the bride to make for the groom on the occasion of their wedding. In everyday life, it is sometimes the main dish for an evening meal, served with salty, thin slices of dried beef or sausage. Toppings can be fruit-juice syrup, cold sweet milk, or—best of all—a pouring of melted butter and a sprinkling of cinnamon sugar.

NORWEGIAN SOUR CREAM PORRIDGE
(*Römmegröt*)

1 *cup commercial sour cream*	1 *teaspoon sugar*
	¾ *teaspoon salt*
1 *tablespoon quick-cooking hot wheat cereal*	3 *tablespoons melted butter*
	½ *cup sugar*
2 *cups milk*	1 *teaspoon cinnamon*

In a saucepan, simmer sour cream 3 minutes, stirring. Mix the wheat cereal with a little of the milk to make a smooth paste; beat into sour cream. Gradually stir in milk, sugar, and salt, cooking and stirring until soup is smooth and thickened. Ladle soup into warm bowls. Pour melted butter over soup and sprinkle with sugar mixed with cinnamon. *Makes 4 servings.*

Through our rain-spattered windshield we first viewed the thriving port city of Bergen. A damp excursion through the bustling open-air fish market turned up a chattery new acquaintance, the bearer of just enough self-esteem to describe herself as a "good cooker." She told us how to cook a fabulous whale dish—but more to the point, veal steaks, Norwegian style, and a winter soup.

VEAL STEAKS IN SOUR CREAM

1 small onion, finely chopped	Pepper
¼ cup butter	1 cup commercial sour cream
4 veal steaks	½ cup shredded Gjetost
Salt	(Norwegian goat cheese)

In a large frying pan, sauté onion in about 1½ tablespoons of the butter until golden; remove from frying pan; set aside. Season veal steaks with salt and pepper to taste. Melt remaining butter in frying pan; add veal and sauté over medium heat on both sides until golden brown and tender. Remove meat from pan; keep warm. Return onions to frying pan; reduce heat to low. Add sour cream and shredded cheese; heat and stir until cheese melts. Return veal to frying pan and spoon sauce over it; heat through. *Makes 4 servings.*

WINTER VEGETABLE SOUP

1 medium-sized onion, chopped	1 large turnip, peeled and cut into crosswise slices about ¼-inch thick
1½ tablespoons butter	3 cups water
¼ pound smoked link sausages (about 4 links), cut into ¼-inch thick diagonal slices	¾ teaspoon salt
	⅛ teaspoon each dried thyme and pepper
3 carrots, peeled and cut into match-like sticks	1 teaspoon capers (optional)
	Chopped fresh parsley

In a large saucepan, sauté onion in butter until limp. Add sausages and carrots. Cut turnip slices into quarters and add to pan along with water, salt, thyme, and pepper. Cover pan; heat until liquid boils. Reduce heat and simmer 30 minutes or until vegetables are tender. (If you wish, add capers just before serving; heat through.) Sprinkle top of each serving with chopped parsley. *Makes 6 servings.*

Looking down at our "sensible" traveling shoes and stockings sagging around the ankles, we wondered if "those feet" could really be attached to us. The toes of Shirley's pointed-tip blacks had curled up after rainy days' cramming inside plastic rain boots—their elf-like appearance a striking contrast to Barbara's stout Italian oxfords.

From Bergen we ventured north in search of sun, and found it and Solvorn, too. This isolated fjord village was the perfect spot to dry out and to expand our treasury of recipes by two fruit desserts.

In every garden—bushes dripping with plump, red currants—we wondered: for what delectable purpose might these be cultivated? And then we tasted them, hidden beneath a finely foamed vanilla egg sauce.

RED CURRANTS WITH EGGEDOSIS*

3 cups fresh red currants	Pinch of salt
Sugar	½ cup sugar
6 eggs, separated	1½ teaspoons vanilla

Wash currants; remove stems and tails. Sprinkle with sugar to sweeten; very gently stir to mix. Allow currants to stand at room temperature 30 minutes or until syrup forms from currant juice and the sugar. Meanwhile, beat egg whites with salt until foamy. Gradually add sugar, beating until egg whites are stiff but not dry. Beat egg yolks until thick; add vanilla. Gently fold egg whites into yolks. Spoon currants with juice into stemmed dessert glasses, reserving a few currants for garnish. Spoon egg sauce on top of each serving; top with a few currants. *Makes 6 servings.*

Velvet-green hillsides massed with fruit blossoms in the spring-time foretell a full harvest of apples and plums in late

---

* Not a malady, but an aristocratic sauce.

August. Then the Norwegian homemakers of the orchard valleys poach the fruits in a vanilla-spiced syrup.

AUGUST FRUITS COMPOTE, NORWAY

2 *cups sugar*
½ *cup each orange juice and water*
1 *vanilla bean, split*
8 *cooking apples, peeled and sliced in wedges about ¾-inch thick*

16 *fresh yellow plums, halved and pitted (or use well-drained, canned greengage plums)*
About ¾ *cup commercial sour cream*
Ground mace

Combine in a saucepan sugar, orange juice, and water. Scrape seeds from vanilla bean and add seeds and pod to saucepan. Simmer mixture together, stirring occasionally, until clear and syrupy. Remove from heat; strain syrup through a fine sieve or cheesecloth. Return strained syrup to saucepan. Add apples and fresh plums (if using canned plums, do not add now, but add at end of cooking time). Cover saucepan and simmer apples and plums 20 minutes or until almost tender (they should retain their shape). Remove from heat; allow to cool to room temperature. Bring compote to the table in a handsome bowl. Ladle fruits and syrup into individual serving bowls. Pass a bowl of whipped sour cream, lightly dusted with ground mace, for each person to spoon over his serving. *Makes 8 servings.*

At a sedate little inn on the outskirts of Trondheim, we placed an order for two omelets. As Shirley polished off an introductory bowl of soup, an omelet appeared on a serving platter. Barbara ate it. The waiter returned, looked horrified at the sight of Shirley's yet unfilled dinner plate, disappeared. And in the kitchen . . . the cooks snickered . . . reached for another carton of eggs . . . "and you know, that plump one ate the whole thing!"

Our minds stuffed with legends of King Olav, Harald the Fairhair, and Erik of the Bloody Axe, we entered ancient Trondheim. Fru Meinhirdt was the treasure of a cook we met there—and well she might be. For she has had a long career of pleasing people with her cooking—children, grandchildren, foreign diplomats, even a Norwegian ambassador. Throughout a long afternoon visit, she poured forth food ideas.

The King of Norway liked this. He tasted it one time when he paid a call on the ambassador.

NORWEGIAN PAPRIKA CHICKEN

1 *frying chicken (2½ to 3 pounds), cut into serving pieces*
Flour
Garlic salt
Pepper
About ¾ cup (1½ sticks) butter
1 *medium-sized onion, peeled and sliced*
½ *pound mushrooms, sliced*
¼ *cup raisins*
2 *teaspoons paprika*
2¼ *cups chicken stock*
1 *cup heavy cream*
1 *cup regular rice*
Parsley sprigs
Paprika

Coat chicken pieces in flour seasoned with garlic salt and pepper. Melt about ⅓ cup of the butter in a heavy frying pan, quickly brown chicken pieces on all sides, remove from frying pan, set aside. In same frying pan, melt 2 tablespoons more of the butter, add mushrooms and raisins, heat and turn just until coated with butter, remove from pan, set aside. Add 2 tablespoons more of the butter to frying pan, add onion slices, and sauté just until limp. Arrange chicken pieces over onions. Sprinkle with the 2 teaspoons paprika. Sprinkle mushrooms and raisins over chicken. Add ¼ cup of the chicken stock and the cream. Cover pan. Simmer chicken 45 minutes or until very tender, basting occasionally with juices in bottom of pan. Meanwhile, in a saucepan, heat and stir rice in 2 tablespoons butter until toasted. Add the remaining 2 cups chicken stock; cover pan and cook rice until tender, about 20 minutes. At serving time, turn rice onto heated platter. Arrange chicken and sauce on top of rice. Garnish platter with parsley sprigs and a dusting of paprika. *Makes 4 to 6 servings.*

CHEESE-BAKED SPINACH
AND TOMATOES

4 *slices bacon*
1 *pound fresh spinach (or 1*   3 *medium-sized tomatoes,*
    package, 12-ounce size,   *peeled and sliced*
    frozen spinach leaves)   ¼ *pound Swiss cheese, sliced*
Salt and Pepper

Cut bacon into 2-inch pieces. Cook until crisp; drain on absorbent paper. Wash fresh spinach thoroughly; shake off excess moisture; remove tough stems. (Or pour boiling water over frozen spinach to thaw it slightly; break apart with fork; drain thoroughly.) Arrange spinach over bottom of a greased, shallow baking-and-serving dish (about 1½-quart size). Sprinkle spinach with salt and pepper to taste. Arrange tomato slices in a single layer, in a decorative pattern, over top of spinach; sprinkle with salt and pepper. Arrange cheese slices between tomato slices to cover spinach. Sprinkle bacon over top. Bake, uncovered, in a moderately hot oven (375°) for 20 minutes or until cheese is melted and spinach is tender. *Makes 6 servings.*

This is a party dish. In fact it's called "Special Fish." Fru Meinhirdt sets rolled fillets of sole around a mound of green asparagus tips. Wine and butter take on cream and shrimp to become the gilding.

SPECIAL FISH

4 sole fillets	1 tablespoon flour
Salt	1 cup light cream
Pepper	½ pound (about 1 cup) tiny
¼ cup (½ stick) butter,	cooked shrimp
melted	About 1½ cups cooked
About ⅔ cup dry white table	asparagus tips
wine	

Sprinkle sole fillets on both sides with salt and pepper to taste. Cut each fillet in half, lengthwise. Roll; fasten with a toothpick. Set rolls on end, close together, in a saucepan. Pour melted butter over rolls. Pour into saucepan enough wine just to cover fish. Cover pan and simmer just until fish flakes easily with a fork, about 10 minutes. Pour liquid into another pan. Keep fish warm. Heat poaching liquid to boiling. Quickly beat in a smooth paste made by mixing flour with a little of the cream. Gradually add remaining cream. Cook and stir until smooth and slightly thickened. Season sauce with salt and pepper. Fold in shrimp; heat through. At serving time, place asparagus in center of warm serving platter. Remove toothpicks from sole rolls and place around asparagus. Serve fish and asparagus from platter. Pass hot shrimp sauce separately. *Makes 4 servings.*

If you're a fancier of apples with pork, bake browned pork chops on a bed of juicy caraway apples. Crown each chop with a glowing baked half apple.

CARAWAY PORK CHOPS AND APPLES

6 pork chops, ½-inch thick	*2 tablespoons butter*
Salt	*9 apples, halved and cored*
Pepper	*1 teaspoon caraway seeds*
Powdered sage	

Sprinkle pork chops with salt, pepper, and sage to taste. In a frying pan, quickly brown chops on both sides in melted butter. Arrange 12 of the apple halves, slightly overlapping, cut side up, in bottom of greased baking dish (about 9 by 13 inches). Sprinkle apples with caraway seeds. Arrange browned chops in a single layer over apples. Prick remaining apple halves with fork. Top each chop with one apple half, placed cut side down. Scrape drippings from frying pan and pour over apples and chops. Cover pan and bake in moderately hot oven (375°) for 25 minutes. Twice during baking, remove cover and baste apples with juice in bottom of baking dish. Remove cover and bake 10 minutes more or until apples and chops are tender. *Makes 6 servings.*

You might try Fru Meinhirdt's Norwegian blueberry omelet for dessert or a festive breakfast. Sugar crystals melt, caramelize, and glisten with fresh-grated lemon peel to make a crisp sugar crusting on a fluffy omelet. Over the top, pour a hot blueberry sauce.

NORWEGIAN BLUEBERRY OMELET

4 *eggs, separated*	¼ *cup sugar*
¼ *cup cream or milk*	1 *teaspoon grated lemon peel*
¼ *teaspoon salt*	*Hot Blueberry Sauce (recipe*
2 *tablespoons butter*	*below)*

Beat egg whites until stiff but not dry; set aside. In a large mixing bowl, beat egg yolks until thick and lemon-colored. Beat in cream and salt. Fold in beaten egg whites. Melt butter in heavy frying pan (about 9-inch diameter); turn in eggs. Turn heat to low. Cook very slowly until eggs are golden brown on bottom (about 10 minutes). Place in moderate oven (350°), and bake about 10 minutes or until knife inserted in center comes out clean. Loosen omelet from pan. Cut across center. Fold omelet, and turn out onto serving platter. Sprinkle top with sugar mixed with lemon peel. Slip under broiler for a few moments until sugar melts and browns slightly. Pour some of the blueberry sauce over omelet. Serve immediately. Pass remaining blueberry sauce. *Makes 3 to 4 servings.*

Hot Blueberry Sauce: Combine in a saucepan 1½ cups fresh blueberries (or 1 package, 10-ounce size, frozen blueberries), ½ cup water, 2 tablespoons lemon juice, ⅛ teaspoon salt, and a dash of cinnamon. Stir together ⅔ cup sugar and 1 tablespoon cornstarch; add to blueberry mixture. Cook over moderate heat, stirring until sauce is thickened and smooth.

These fried apples are for dessert.

FRIED APPLE RINGS WITH SUGAR-BUTTERED ALMONDS

¼ cup sugar	*5 tablespoons butter*
¼ teaspoon powdered ginger	*3 apples, cored and sliced in*
¼ cup slivered almonds	*¼-inch-thick rings*

Mix sugar and ginger. Sauté almonds in 1 tablespoon of the butter until toasted; stir in half the sugar-ginger mixture; set aside and keep warm. In a large frying pan with cover, melt remaining butter. Add apple slices and sprinkle with remaining sugar-ginger mixture. Cover pan and cook apples over medium heat until almost tender, about 10 minutes. With flexible spatula, carefully turn apples and cook on second side until tender. Arrange about 4 apple rings in a row, overlapping, on each of 4 warm dessert plates. Sprinkle almonds in a line down center of apple rings. Spoon any remaining pan juices over apples. *Makes 4 servings.*

Through a long life and wide experience, Fru Meinhirdt has become well acquainted with the pattern of life in rural Norway. She told us that Norwegian country wives stir up this omelet when their husbands come home late from a hard day in the field. Hence its name, Farmer's Omelet. Double or triple the recipe and cook it in a bigger frying pan if you want to serve more than one . . . (husband?)

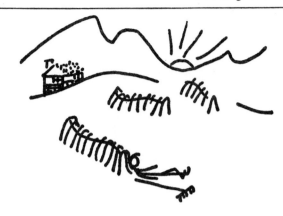

FARMER'S OMELET
(*Bonde Omelet*)

2 *strips bacon, cut into 2-inch pieces*	*into 1½-inch lengths*
	2 *eggs*
½ *medium-sized potato, very thinly sliced*	2 *tablespoons cream or milk*
	Salt
1 *green onion with top, cut*	*Pepper*

In a medium-sized frying pan (about 8 inches in diameter) cook bacon and potato, turning frequently until both are very crisp. Pour off all but about 1 tablespoon bacon fat. Cut onion pieces into very thin slivers, lengthwise. Reserve a few onion strips for garnish; add remaining onions to frying pan. Heat and stir a few moments. Beat eggs with cream and salt and pepper to taste, and pour over contents of frying pan, rotating pan so egg covers bottom. Cook over low heat, lifting egg and tilting pan to let the uncooked egg flow to bottom of pan. When egg is set on bottom, still moist on top, fold as for a regular French omelet and turn out of pan onto a warm plate. Sprinkle with reserved green onions. *Makes 1 supper serving.*

Fru Meinhirdt's neighbor joined us for afternoon tea and told of two soups. A light, hot soup is often her ruse to whet appetites for a bountiful meal.

LEMON-CARROT BOUILLON

2 cups beef bouillon
2 small carrots, peeled and very thinly sliced
4 very thin slices lemon

2 teaspoons lemon juice
3 tablespoons chopped fresh parsley

Combine in a saucepan the bouillon, carrots, lemon slices and juice, and 2 tablespoons of the parsley. Cover and cook for 15 minutes or just until carrots are tender. Serve soup immediately, ladling a lemon slice into each individual bowl. Sprinkle a little fresh parsley on top of each serving. *Makes 4 servings.*

Serve this nourishing soup with a pat of butter melting on top of each bowlful—and a sprinkling of dill and nutmeg.

SUMMER-VEGETABLES CREAM SOUP

1 small head cauliflower
4 carrots, peeled and sliced
2 cups green beans, cut into 2-inch pieces
2 cups green peas
¼ pound cooked smoked ham, finely diced
1½ teaspoon salt
½ teaspoon sugar
2½ cups water

6 tablespoons each butter and flour
2 cups milk
1 teaspoon salt
¼ teaspoon ground nutmeg
1 egg yolk, beaten
Butter
Dried dill weed
Additional nutmeg

Break cauliflower into small flowerets. Place in a large kettle with carrots, beans, peas, ham, salt, sugar, and water. Cover and gently boil just until vegetables are tender. Drain vegetables, saving cooking liquid. Melt the 6 tablespoons butter in a saucepan. Stir in flour to make a smooth paste. Gradually add milk, cooking and stirring to make a smooth sauce. Gradually add liquid remaining from cooking vegetables, salt, and nutmeg. Stir a little of the hot liquid into egg yolk. Gradually add egg mixture to soup liquid in saucepan, beating briskly. Add cooked vegetables and heat thoroughly. Ladle into hot soup bowls. Top each serving with a thin pat of butter and a light sprinkling *each* of dill weed and nutmeg. *Makes 8 servings.*

Shirley had to take a bus from Fru Meinhirdt's country home back to Trondheim to see Fru Fassa. Trying desperately to get directions from a "monolingual" Norwegian, she pleaded, "Well, if you don't speak English, do you know anyone who does?"

The cream cakes in Norway are sweet wonders! Fru Fassa began her dissertation on food with a discourse on combinations of cake layers, fillings, frostings, and flavorings. Yet one of the best cakes is one of the simplest.

NORWEGIAN CREAM CAKE

1½ cups (3 sticks) soft
  butter
2 cups sugar
3 eggs
1½ cups commercial sour
  cream
1½ teaspoons vanilla
3 cups all-purpose flour
2¼ teaspoons baking powder
¾ teaspoon baking soda

⅜ teaspoon salt
1 cup heavy cream
⅓ cup brown sugar, firmly
  packed
½ teaspoon vanilla
½ cup chopped walnuts
1 tablespoon sifted brown
  sugar
Walnut halves

In a large mixing bowl, cream together thoroughly butter and the 2 cups sugar. Beat in eggs, one at a time; beat until mixture is light and fluffy. Beat in sour cream and the 1½ teaspoons vanilla. Sift flour, measure, and sift again with baking powder, soda, and salt. Gradually add to creamed mixture; beat to blend thoroughly. Divide batter evenly among 3 greased 9-inch round cake pans. Bake in a moderate oven (350°) for 45 minutes or until cake pulls away from sides of pan and toothpick inserted in center comes out clean. Allow cake layers to cool in pan a few minutes; then turn out on wire racks to cool thoroughly. Whip cream with the ⅓ cup brown sugar and the ½ teaspoon vanilla. To assemble cake, place one layer on platter; spread top completely to edges with one third of the whipped cream. Sprinkle with half the chopped walnuts. Top with another cake layer; repeat with spreading of cream and nuts. Top with third layer; spread remaining cream over top. Sprinkle with the 1 tablespoon sifted brown sugar; decorate with walnut halves. *Makes 12 to 16 servings.*

From cakes we moved on to chicken. Fru Fassa proposes butter-browned chicken steamed with dried fruits, and further suggests hot cheese biscuits. (Just bake your best flaky baking-powder biscuits, but first, stir into the dough ½ cup shredded sharp cheese for every 1 cup flour.)

FRUITED LEMON CHICKEN

⅓ cup butter	*Pepper*
¼ cup halved filberts	*Pinch of crumbled dried*
1 frying chicken (about 2½	*thyme*
pounds), cut into serving	*½ lemon, sliced*
pieces	*10 moist dried prunes*
Salt	*½ cup dried apricots*

Melt butter in a large frying pan. Add filberts; heat and stir until nuts are lightly toasted; remove from pan and set aside. Season chicken pieces with salt and pepper. Cook in butter in frying pan until brown on all sides, about 20 minutes. Reduce heat. Sprinkle chicken with thyme. Arrange lemon slices, prunes, and apricots over top of chicken. Cover chicken and cook 30 minutes more. Remove cover, add filberts, and cook chicken, uncovered, 5 minutes more or until tender. Arrange chicken and fruits on warm serving platter. Pour any remaining pan dripping over top. *Makes 4 to 6 servings.*

When recipe reconnaissance led us to the door of Fru Hanger, we were assailed by that miracle aroma—fresh bread baking. Fru Hanger is a rotund lady, who must surely bake the best breads in Norway.

NORWEGIAN HERB WHOLE-WHEAT BREAD

1 package yeast (active dry or compressed)
2 tablespoons water (warm for dry yeast, lukewarm for compressed)
½ cup milk
¼ cup sugar
¼ cup shortening
1 teaspoon salt
1½ cups whole-wheat flour
3 tablespoons cracked wheat
1 egg, beaten
½ teaspoon nutmeg
¼ teaspoon each crumbled dried thyme, sweet basil, and oregano
About ¾ cup all-purpose flour
Melted butter

Soften yeast in water. Scald milk; pour over sugar, shortening, and salt in a large mixing bowl. Stir to melt shortening and dissolve sugar. When milk mixture has cooled to lukewarm, stir in 1 cup of the whole-wheat flour and cracked wheat. Beat 2 minutes. Add beaten egg, dissolved yeast mixture, nutmeg, thyme, sweet basil, and oregano. Beat well. Stir in the remaining whole-wheat flour and enough all-purpose flour to make a soft dough. Turn dough out on lightly floured board and knead until smooth and satiny. Place dough in a greased bowl; cover and let rise in a warm place until light and doubled in bulk (about 1 hour, 15 minutes). Punch down. Shape into a loaf. Place in greased 5- by 9-inch bread-loaf pan. Let rise until doubled in bulk (about 45 minutes). Bake in a moderately hot oven (375°) for 25 to 30 minutes. Turn out of pan onto wire rack; lightly brush top crust with melted butter. *Makes 1 loaf.*

Cloves and caraway send up a tantalizing steam as you peel slice after slice off this butter-layered bread loaf. It looks like a giant lengthwise fan-tan roll. Serve it *hot* with meats or *hot* with jam for breakfast or coffee time.

FANNED CARAWAY LOAF

¼ cup milk	¼ cup soft butter
1 package yeast (active dry or compressed)	2 to 2½ cups flour
	6 tablespoons soft butter
¼ cup water (warm for dry yeast, lukewarm for compressed)	½ teaspoon each whole caraway seeds and powdered cloves
¼ cup sugar	1 egg, beaten
½ teaspoon salt	Caraway seeds
1 egg	

Scald milk; cool to lukewarm. Sprinkle or crumble yeast into water in a mixing bowl; stir to dissolve. Stir in lukewarm milk, sugar, salt, the 1 egg, the ¼ cup soft butter, and 1 cup of the flour. Stir until smooth. Mix in enough more flour to make a soft dough. Turn onto lightly floured board and knead until smooth and elastic, about 4 minutes. Place in greased bowl; cover and allow to rise in a warm place until almost doubled in bulk (about 1½ hours). Punch down; allow dough to rise again until almost doubled in bulk (about 30 minutes). On a lightly floured board, roll dough into a rectangle 8 by 24 inches. Spread with the 6 tablespoons soft butter. Sprinkle with caraway seeds and cloves. With a sharp knife cut rectangle, crosswise, into 5 strips. Stack the 5 strips evenly, one on top of another. Slice stack, crosswise, though all layers into 6 equal strips. Place layered strips, cut side up, side by side, in bottom of greased loaf pan (5 by 9 inches). Cover and allow to rise until light (15 to 20 minutes). Gently brush top of strips with beaten egg. Sprinkle with a few additional caraway seeds. Bake in a hot oven (400°) for 15 minutes or until golden brown. Let loaf cool in pan a few moments. Carefully turn out. Serve hot. *Makes 1 loaf.*

A SMØRREBRØD SAMPLING

Wherever we went, throughout Scandinavia, we reveled in *smørrebrød* of boundless variety. Among all these many-layered open-face sandwiches, we chose five favorites to share with you.

BLUE-CHEESE DESSERT

Spread a thin slice of firm rye bread with soft butter. Cover with a layer of blue cheese. Top with a spoonful of sweet cherry preserves.

FRESH CARROT AND LEMON

Spread a thin slice of rye bread with soft butter. Heap high with finely shredded raw carrots. Center with a raw egg yolk. Place a lemon-slice twist on either side of egg yolk. Offer salt and coarse black pepper.

BACON, TOMATO, CAMEMBERT

Spread a thin slice of sour rye bread (with caraway seeds) with butter. Cover with several layers of very crisp bacon slices. Top with alternating rows of thin tomato slices and slices of ripe Camembert cheese (with crust).

RARE ROAST BEEF

Spread a piece of Scandinavian crisp cracker bread (available in specialty food stores and some supermarkets) with soft butter. Cover with rolls of thinly sliced rare roast beef. Top with a layer of thin tomato slices. Sprinkle generously with thin onion slices that have been sautéed in butter until crisp. Garnish with wedges of eggs that have been cooked in simmering water just until yolks are set—not firm.

SMOKED HERRING AND HORSERADISH

Spread a thin slice of firm rye bread with soft butter. Cover with a layer of smoked herring. Top with a little mound of finely chopped mild onions, another mound of curls of fresh horseradish, and a cluster of watercress. Center *smørrebrød* with a raw egg yolk served in the half shell of an egg.

INDEX

INDEX

Scandinavian Interest Books from Hippocrene . . .

GOOD FOOD FROM SWEDEN
Inga Norberg
This classic of Swedish cookery includes recipes for fish and meat dishes, vegetables, breads and sweets, including cookies, cakes candies and syrups. A large section is dedicated to the savory tidbits included in the traditional Swedish smorgasbord.
192 pages • 5½ x 8¼ • 0-7818-0486-8 • $10.95pb • (544)

THE BEST OF SMORGASBORD COOKING
Gerda Simonson
Recipes for the traditional Swedish smorgasbord, including meat and game dishes, aspics and salads, fish, pastas and vegetables.
158 pages • 5½ x 8¼ • 0-7818-0407-8 • $14.95pb • (207)

TREASURY OF FINNISH LOVE POEMS, QUOTATIONS & PROVERBS
In Finnish and English
Börje Vähämäki, editor and translator
128 pages • 5 x 7 • 0-7818-0397-7 • $11.95hc • (118)

NORSE STORIES
Hamilton Wright Mabie
Stories of brave warriors, fierce gods, and exciting adventures included in such tales as "Odin's Search for Wisdom," "Thor Goes a Fishing," "How Thor Fought the Giant Hrungner" and "The Twilight of the Gods" will enchant children and adults alike.
250 pages • 5½ x 8¼ • Illustrations • 0-7818-0770-0 • $14.95hc • (357)

SWEDISH FAIRY TALES
Translated by H. L. Braekstad
A unique blend of enchantment, adventure, comedy, and romance make this collection of Swedish fairy tales a must-have for any library. With 18 different, classic Swedish fairy tales and 21 beautiful black-and-white illustrations, this is an ideal gift for children and adults alike.
190 pages • 5½ x 8¼ • 21 b/w illustrations • 0-7818-0717-4 • $12.50hc • (787)

HIPPOCRENE CHILDREN'S ILLUSTRATED SWEDISH DICTIONARY
English-Swedish/Swedish-English

This children's picture dictionary includes 500 words in English and Swedish (with pronunciation), each accompanied by a large color illustration.

94 pages • 8½ x 11 • 0-7818-0822-7 • $14.95hc • (57)

MASTERING FINNISH, REVISED EDITION
Börje Vähämäki

288 pages • 6 x 9 • 0-7818-0800-6 • $16.95pb • (184)

FINNISH-ENGLISH/ENGLISH-FINNISH CONCISE DICTIONARY

12,000 entries • 411 pages • 3½ x 4¾ • 0-87052-813-0 • $11.95pb • (142)

ENGLISH-NORWEGIAN/NORWEGIAN-ENGLISH CONCISE DICTIONARY

600 pages • 3⅝ x 5⅜ • 0-7818-0199-0 • $14.95pb • (202)

DANISH-ENGLISH/ENGLISH-DANISH PRACTICAL DICTIONARY

32,000 entries • 601 pages • 4⅜ x 7 • 0-87052-823-8 • $16.95pb • (198)

SWEDISH-ENGLISH/ENGLISH-SWEDISH STANDARD DICTIONARY

70,000 entries • 804 pages • 5½ x 8½ • 0-7818-0379-9 • $19.95pb • (242)